FORGING THE FUTURE
of
SPECIAL COLLECTIONS

ALA Neal-Schuman purchases fund advocacy, awareness, and accreditation programs for library professionals worldwide.

Forging the Future of Special Collections

Edited by
Melissa A. Hubbard, Robert H. Jackson,
and Arnold Hirshon

CHICAGO 2016

© 2016 by the American Library Association

Extensive effort has gone into ensuring the reliability of the information in this book; however, the publisher makes no warranty, express or implied, with respect to the material contained herein.

ISBNs
978-0-8389-1386-4 (paper)
978-0-8389-1422-9 (PDF)
978-0-8389-1423-6 (ePub)
978-0-8389-1424-3 (Kindle)

Library of Congress Cataloging-in-Publication Data
Names: Hubbard, Melissa A., editor. | Jackson, Robert H., 1936- editor. | Hirshon, Arnold, 1950- editor.
Title: Forging the future of special collections / edited by Melissa A. Hubbard, Robert H. Jackson, Arnold Hirshon.
Description: Chicago : ALA Neal-Schuman, an imprint of the American Library Association, 2016. | "This book grew out of a colloquium on 'Forging the Future of Special Collections,' which was held in October 2014 and organized by the Kelvin Smith Library at Case Western Reserve University, Cleveland, Ohio. The colloquium evolved from a Rare Book Forum at the Library of Congress that was given in 2001, called 'Private Collectors and Special Collections Libraries,' which was organized by Mark Dimunation, Chief of the Rare Book and Special Collections Division at the Library of Congress, and aided by Dan DeSimone"--Introduction. | Includes bibliographical references and index.
Identifiers: LCCN 2015040003 | ISBN 9780838913864 (print : alk. paper)
Subjects: LCSH: Libraries--United States--Special collections. | Libraries--Special collections--Forecasting. | Rare book libraries--United States. | Academic libraries--United States. | Library materials--Digitization. | Libraries--Gifts, legacies.
Classification: LCC Z688.A3 U63 2016 | DDC 026--dc23 LC record available at http://lccn.loc.gov/2015040003

Cover design by Alejandra Diaz. Imagery © Shutterstock, Inc. Text design and composition by Mayfly Design in the Garamond Premier Pro and Gotham typefaces.

♾ This paper meets the requirements of ANSI/NISO Z39.48–1992 (Permanence of Paper).
Printed in the United States of America

20 19 18 17 16   5 4 3 2 1

Dedicated to Robert H. Jackson, library friend and distinguished scholar, who inspired this book and the 2014 colloquium upon which it is based.

In memory of Paul T. Ruxin (1943–2016), whose contribution to this book is an enduring aide-mémoire of his erudition and grace.

Contents

Preface, *by Arnold Hirshon* xi
Introduction, *by Robert H. Jackson* xiii

Part I	Communities

CHAPTER 1   Reflections on the Meanings of Objects 3
E. Haven Hawley

CHAPTER 2   Affinities and Alliances: Thoughts on Acquisitions, Collection Development, and Donor Relations 11
Jim Kuhn

CHAPTER 3   Where Does the Collector/Donor Community See Special Collections Today? 31
Jon A. Lindseth

CHAPTER 4   Collecting Communities: The Role of Special Collections Librarians and Archivists in Creating New Life for Community-Based Collections 37
Melissa A. Hubbard

CHAPTER 5   The Role of the Auction House 45
Selby Kiffer

CHAPTER 6   Forging into the Future: Facing Digital Realities and Forecasting Endeavors for Special Collections Librarianship 53
Athena N. Jackson

Part II	The Enduring Object

CHAPTER 7 Lawrence Clark Powell Revisited: The Functions of Rare Books Today 63
Joel Silver

CHAPTER 8 Special Collections Libraries and the Uses of the Past (Apologies to Herbert Muller) 67
Paul Ruxin

CHAPTER 9 Everything Old Is New Again: Transformation in Special Collections 73
Alice Schreyer

CHAPTER 10 Special Collections and the Booksellers of Today . . 85
Tom Congalton

CHAPTER 11 Acknowledging the Past 89
Daniel De Simone

CHAPTER 12 Literary Archives: How They Have Changed and How They Are Changing 95
Ken Lopez

CHAPTER 13 Objects of Study: Special Collections in an Age of Digital Scholarship 101
Stephen Enniss

| **Part III** | **From Periphery to Center** |

CHAPTER 14 Considering the Present: Special Collections Are the Meal, Not the Dessert 117
Jay Satterfield

CHAPTER 15 Teaching with Special Collections 131
Christoph Irmscher

CHAPTER 16 From Siberia to Shangri-La 157
Sarah Thomas

CHAPTER 17 The Once and Future Special Collections 167
Mark Dimunation

About the Editors and Contributors 187

Index 193

Preface

On October 21 and 22 of 2014, the Kelvin Smith Library of Case Western Reserve University organized and hosted a colloquium on the past, present, and future of special collections in libraries. At that highly successful event there were over 200 librarians, booksellers, book collectors, donors, and auction house representatives in attendance who came from nineteen states of the United States and two provinces in Canada. We believe the colloquium was a milestone event in assessing the past and projecting the future of special collections.

This book, while motivated by the excellent presentations given during the colloquium, stands apart from it, organized not chronologically around past, present, and future, but rather around a new set of themes. In addition, many of the authors have expanded significantly upon their original remarks. Nonetheless, you as the reader are likely to detect a bit of the flavor (and sense the excitement) of the original colloquium in each of the chapters.

No colloquium nor publication such as this is the work of a single individual. As one of the co-organizers and coeditors, I would also like to express particular thanks to some of the people who provided guidance and support along the way.

The cochairs of the colloquium, who are also now the coeditors of this publication, benefitted greatly from the work of a Planning Committee, whose members included Michael Clune (Associate Professor, English, Case Western Reserve University); Daniel Cohen (Associate Professor, History and Art, Case Western Reserve University); Jenifer Neils (Elsie B. Smith Professor in the Liberal Arts, Case Western Reserve University); Alice Schreyer (then at the University of Chicago, and now the Roger and Julie Baskes Vice President for Collections and Library Services at the Newberry Library); Joel Silver (Director and Curator of Books, Lilly Library, Indiana University Bloomington); and Jill Tatem (University Archivist, Case Western Reserve University).

Preface

I am also greatly appreciative of the support of the three collaborating partner universities that launched the colloquium, and their superb library directors: Mary Ann Mavrinac at the University of Rochester River Campus Libraries, Joseph (Jody) Combs at the Vanderbilt University Libraries, and my longtime colleague and good friend, Jeffrey Trzeciak at the Washington University in St. Louis Libraries. In addition to the very generous sponsors who made the original colloquium possible, I want to give very special thanks to our extraordinary staff at the Kelvin Smith Library, and particularly Gina Midlik, Angela Sloan, and Melissa Hubbard and the continuing members of her Special Collections and Archives Team: Nora Blackman, Helen Conger, Sharlane Gubkin, and Jill Tatem. It is these people and my other Kelvin Smith Library colleagues—too numerous to mention—who make coming to work each day such a delight.

One final personal note: I cannot thank enough my friend, colleague, and mentor in this endeavor, Robert H. Jackson, the Distinguished Visiting Scholar of the Kelvin Smith Library. It was his inspiration and constant encouragement that caused us not only to convene the colloquium, but to pursue publication of these very important essays.

I know you will find this book to be thought-provoking as we as a profession continue to forge the future of special collections.

Arnold Hirshon
Associate Provost and University Librarian
Case Western Reserve University

INTRODUCTION

Forging the Future

ROBERT H. JACKSON

This book grew out of a colloquium on special collections entitled "Acknowledging the Past, Forging the Future," which was held in October 2014 and organized by the Kelvin Smith Library at Case Western Reserve University, Cleveland, Ohio. The colloquium evolved from a Rare Book Forum at the Library of Congress that was given in April 2001, "Private Collectors and Special Collections Libraries," which was organized by Mark Dimunation, Chief of the Rare Book and Special Collections Division at the Library of Congress, aided by Dan De Simone. It turned out to be a very special occasion as librarians, book dealers, and collectors came together and exchanged a great deal of valuable information. The speakers on that program were Alice Schreyer, William Reese, and myself, and there were several panels.

In 2001, my talk, "Will the Collector of Today Be the Donor of Tomorrow?"[1] seemed to hit a nerve. We were at the turn of the century. There was anxiety about the future of collecting, the future of rare book libraries, and the future of the book itself.

That was the heyday of the printed book, with millions of books coming off the presses every year. At the same time, things were about to change. The Internet opened up new horizons in book sales, but it was also stepping up the pace of digitization. Writers no longer had any use for handwritten manuscripts, typescripts, or the kind of notes and ephemera that formed the backbone of author archives. I noted that a page of manuscript in Charles Dickens's own hand (from my own collection) was an example of what would be lost, and with that the loss of insight that we gain from seeing revisions, additions, and the occasional ink blot or coffee stain.

I commented then that the field of book collecting had changed drastically in recent years. Book collectors were younger, more heterogeneous, and less clubby than their predecessors. Books and ephemera that were once considered marginal were now moving to center stage. I described the rise of library special collections, and their changing fortunes. At one time, libraries were the dominant purchasers of rare books, but by 2001 they were becoming more and more dependent on donors and endowments to fill out their collections.

I concluded that in the future, special collections libraries would need to act like other successful nonprofit organizations. They would need to assess their wants, survey the pool of potential donors, and target those individuals whose collections complement their own. They would need to build relationships of trust that would stimulate collectors' altruistic impulses.

Today, we're living in the future we speculated about in 2001. Many of the trends identified then have come to pass. The digitization of culture has been relentless. The ebook is now mainstream. The physical book persists, but it is far from the center of culture. Handwriting itself is on the way out, and the smart phone is the central fact of modern life. Library special collections continue to straddle the world between digital phenomena and the world of physical objects. All that is solid melts into air.

Now we are forced back to the existential questions. What is a book? What is it good for? Why do we collect and preserve books? Who's interested in our special collections and who will use them in years to come?

Since 2001, the market for rare books and manuscripts has changed a great deal. The canonical works and their associated manuscripts are off the market. The Internet leveled the playing field, and the middle ground of collecting has been devalued, and lost much of its excitement and appeal.

Author archives used to be purchased by private collectors. My own collection has included several major archives, but this is becoming rarer. Authors and their descendants today are donating or selling their archives to libraries and special collections. Today's private collectors are looking for something more rare and wonderful—their own private "blockbusters" that will create talk and publicity.

Introduction

The sheer volume of information available online means that today's librarians have the opportunity to be more knowledgeable and better trained than ever. However, those who have been trained in the digital era are increasingly oriented to the digital world. Special collections may be losing their edge in the field of unique and rare books, and in the long-run special collections may suffer.

I stand by the original conclusion of my 2001 talk. The future of special collections is a matter of building and nurturing relationships between librarians and collectors. The more we learn about one another, the more we can help each other achieve our goals.

The papers contained in this book, which were inspired by the Kelvin Smith Library colloquium in 2014, are part of the process of redefinition and renewal. We chose to call this "Forging the Future" *not* "Waiting for the Future" nor "Wondering about the Future." The implication is that the future is in our hands. We will control it. We will shape it. The decisions we make as readers, collectors, and special librarians today will determine what happens to our fields tomorrow. This is a hopeful message, and this book presents a hopeful future as well.

The 2014 "Forging the Future" colloquium appealed to a national audience and videos of the colloquium were watched extensively online.[2] This book expands and enriches the ideas presented at the colloquium by including significant additional material from the contributors. The chapters are thoughtful, insightful, and provocative.

We are in the early stages of what Stephen J. Gould called "punctuated evolution" for special collections. Although it may be difficult to predict, I believe this book will demonstrate that special collections has a vigorous and lively future.

NOTES

1. Robert H. Jackson, "Will the Collector of Today Be the Donor of Tomorrow?," in *Book Talk: Essays on Books, Book Sellers, Collecting, and Special Collections*, ed. Robert H. Jackson and Carol Zeman Rothkopf (New Castle, DE: Oak Knoll Press, 2006).
2. The videos of the 2014 colloquium can be found at https://www.youtube.com/playlist?list=PLBELrG1nZ2U5jXND2u48h4RScCZwngM5g.

PART I

Communities

The traditional relationships between collectors, booksellers, librarians, and archivists are changing rapidly.

PART 1

Commentaries

CHAPTER 1

Reflections on the Meanings of Objects

E. HAVEN HAWLEY

Memories help us to make sense of the trajectories in which we live our lives. They anchor us in a changing and difficult world. What a person remembers from the mass of details saturating a specific moment, how he or she selects and places into long-term memory the pertinent facts of that moment, and how those memories are recalled and reconstituted over time, make for significant parallels with the mission of special collections in research libraries.

At the same time, the stories that a community attaches to historical objects and uses to hold itself together over time often are at odds with what special collections do with those objects. I have worked closely with communities in the preservation of cultural heritage, and this fact has permeated the way that I approach and undertake my work, even as the parallels between processes of interpretation over time clearly exist. In this short essay, I offer a few reflections on the meanings of objects in special collections, especially as they relate to memory, authenticity, and social practice. Our authority as stewards of cultural heritage increasingly stems from close connections with lived experience, and collecting community artifacts challenges older practices of evidence and order.

The processes of finding meaning in an artifact such as a book, sheet music, or military medal, of discerning the social configurations and agreements that are part of how we relate to artifacts, exist alongside our mastery of any intellectual content. It is fair to say that these processes are more important than the object itself. We must analyze and interpret them, because the object cannot speak for itself.

An artifact matters, but not in the ways that we or donors often think it does. I know this because when someone hands me a brochure or a business card, I tend not to focus on the text. I'm very polite and make sure that I look at the name and the title. But when I look at your card, I'm primarily examining the printing process and figuring out how many people touched it, and in what ways, before you handed it to me. The writers, designers, and printers are the most obvious of those people. A printer measures samples off the press, and a bindery worker sets up the folding machine just right to make that gatefold work. Someone clamps and cuts those business cards (or, these days, more likely picks them up from the in-office printer, rubber bands a stack, and delivers the bundle to you).

I think of these processes because I have done most of them myself. I visualize the working out of production steps when you may think I'm reading the words printed on the card. It is much easier to be aware of each step and the hands that have made a thing possible when you see yourself, somehow, embedded in that document. My valuing of the card has relatively little to do with the text. Thick or medium-weight, one-color printing or embossed, the card tells me a story about each of the locations in which decisions about it were made, as well as the level of skill and the decision making of each person involved.

You certainly intend to convey your work title and institutional association with the card. You may expect that a recipient values the heavier cardstock and elegance, and often our understandings in that regard would coincide. I am aware of the conventions that your designer relied upon in aligning materiality with institutional prestige. And I would certainly exaggerate if I said that the text mattered not at all.

As communities, printers and book people have an advantage in the assessment of our place in history. We have had good control over the stories that are told about us, primarily because we have conceptualized and undertaken production of those narratives ourselves. We have glorified our work through romantic visions of printing shops, emphasizing the independence of printers, and enhancing the profession's artfulness. In reality, printing is a dirty, nasty occupation. If we allowed others to tell the history of printing and our place in it, that would be more widely known and the act of printing less valorized. In the hand-press era, common printers could be identified on the street by their lurching strides, developed from the constant and uneven strain upon their shoulders, backs, and legs as they daily pulled the bar of the press. We rarely think of misshapen printers when we make printers' hats or purchase a rare broadside. But that is whose history we are actually collecting.

We have, instead, created stories about objects more from the context in which their continuity has been assured than from something inherent in the physical forms. Repositories have collected broadsides or the books of printers who are noted for success, when the object itself is prized. When the focus turns to literature, acquisitions have often reflected a highly refined view of the past. Retrospective selection emphasizes meaning to us in a later generation more than the past as it was. There is far less failure in historical collections of printing and literature than should have been recorded. The selection process rarely positions us, as professionals or those documenting our own kind, at the bottom of a social hierarchy.

And so we might ask: Whose hands touched this book before it came into our possession, and how? What experiences have been enabled and what meanings facilitated by its materiality over time? What does inclusion in special collections, and particularly the transfer of materials to institutions with no direct connection to creators, mean? We need to consider these things in order to negotiate the "object-ness"—or "object-ivity"—of an artifact.

We know that materiality is tied to meaning, but it is difficult to suss out just how that happens. One of my favorite things to do when teaching is to give students a printed object that is older than their great-great-grandparents and let them sit with it. I have yet to meet a student who did not come away with a sense of awe at how long that book has existed. They feel a connection with the past through this artifact, although the object cannot articulate its own meaning. The heft of an object and sense of solidity, smells and what students imagine them to resemble, or marks of apparent age provide cultural clues by which they intuit a possible past.

A book as artifact has, in its words, images, and signs of wear, something that represents continuity over time. The date, characteristics of style, and marks of its passage through hands indicate its age. They echo what some students have read, been taught, or otherwise experienced about things that endure. All of this makes one think that the past is, indeed, a strange place, but one with outlines that are somehow familiar. These books are ghosts on a cultural landscape: material, yes, but meaningful. They are embodiments of the social practices that frame a student's world, created in the past and lingering through the complicity of those in the present.

The immediate experience of holding a book can generate memories specific to the item at hand: its smell, the worn and stained book cloth, a recollection of having held and read novels before, engrossed while rocking in a porch swing. From a host of such recollections and other things learned in deliberate ways over time or breathed in like air from our interactions with those around us, we gain broad knowledge through which we filter and make sense of new experiences. Memory, then, travels intersecting paths between specific episodes and unremembered learning, with what we know about how the world works and our place in it influencing how and what we choose to remember.

At every moment, we take in a wide swath of details from our surroundings. These short-term memories must be translated. We do so retrospectively, selecting elements that seem significant or explanatory, suppressing others. We may, in time, revitalize what becomes relevant to another circumstance. Perhaps we have stood at this street corner before, and we now remember the way home from here. We are always reconstructing our memories, remembering the forgotten, suppressing the no longer useful. Even though a memory seems complete and factual as we recount it, what we articulate about it is mediated by a host of factors, from the bits and pieces that must be reassembled cognitively to reconstruct a full memory to the effects of a changed location.

We can compare the memories of one who offers the object to the processes of an archive. Rather than pulling a complete record of the past from a permanent mental repository, we reassemble the memories we wish to keep from bits stored here and there, available to a variety of memories. Our minds construct plausible bridges across the rocky streams of absent details, aiding us in integrating what we know, have experienced or forgotten, and need imagination to create.

If objects help us to tell stories, we must pay attention to those whose objects are not in collections and whose stories are kept alive by artifacts without textuality. Special collections professionals have a great deal of experience acquiring materials that have already been separated in time from their origins. We are very strong in our connections to traditional collectors, who have done the hard work of assembling coherent collections from the nooks and crannies of auctions, dealer catalogs, out-of-the-way bookstores and, sometimes, serendipity. The elimination of intermediaries between creator and repository fundamentally reshapes long-held acquisition practices of special collections. Engagement now is a cornerstone of cultural authority for the profession.

But the direct transfer of historical materials from creators can be challenging. An artist may refuse to have images released individually, asserting that the *oeuvre* is the only mode of true analysis of his work. The leader of an ethnic group who provides documents may stipulate that they cannot be translated into another language without her permission, because only the mother tongue, as she knows it, can convey concepts correctly. For each of these, the desire to have these objects accepted in their entirety, as assembled and with the same interpretive framework, represents a taxing demand.

An artifact in special collections exists at the juncture of memory and meaning, corroborating the veracity of these reconstructions of what was forgotten or has been pieced together. Like a load-bearing member of a bridge, it appears to be whole and solid, with no need for interpretation, carrying both the past and present. With the help of the associations and experiences that it calls to mind, such an artifact becomes a witness to the seamless truth of our memory.

Its unity serves to explain the intertwined lives of people who shared a book or many books clustered around a way of living and seeing the world, such as religious texts. As an object, a book can be loaded with the freight of the stories of entire communities. Special collections professionals have difficulty when a book, or a set of books, carries more weight than its constituent paper or words. When persistence is its own language, location and context also take on greater meaning. For each person and setting in which these books have existed before they find their way into special collections, they have served as memory markers and makers within contextual circumstances.

To survive physically is less evidence of truthfulness than adaptability to interpretations varying, in large or small ways, from generation to generation. In common, each has said "yes" to the object, however. Objects have meaning because of their continuity. That continuity is a social decision, relating to power and access to resources over time.

We know that a donor or a member of a community viewing a heritage object in a repository brings a different perspective to its interpretation than a scholar with an entirely different emotional and intellectual approach. This relates to social practice. Books as objects and text are conduits of information, and interaction with them is the source of memory. The brain creates memories through the process of selectively retrieving facts and ordering them into useful narratives. Objects have meaning when they are used, not merely because of the continuity of their existence. And it could be argued that without use and the continual construction, sharing, and repeating of memories as stories, objects themselves have no meaning. Therefore they require interaction. Their physicality, smell, textures, and sounds all evoke past experience and collapse time. Ownership can extend beyond physical control and into the realm of a more diffused cultural sense, marked by distinct memories of and recollections triggered by objects. Elements of cultural appropriation remain and may cause ripples on the reconstruction of a donor's related memories.

Could it be that the varied meanings of an object to a donor, a community member, an archivist, or a scholar reflect more than the diverse approaches, expectations, and questions that each brings to engagement? The meaning of an object may change according to its physical location, even for the same person. This involves more than the texture of contemplative encounters, though they are a cherished aspect of how special collections have come to distinguish themselves from research in other surroundings.

The very doorways that we wish to invite people to enter can alter how they remember an object and imagine its role as a part of their own frameworks for memory and meaning. Intriguing new research finds that simply crossing a threshold may disrupt a person's capacity for managing the flow of details fundamental to accurate memory about objects.[1] Experiential assimilation becomes even more complex if the act of traversing physical frames can reset aspects of what we remember about a specific thing. The memory bridge becomes an incomplete cantilever design, ends jutting into a gap between piers but failing to meet. Can such an object testify to the truthfulness of a worldview?

It would be a mistake to see donors as less than full participants in this process. In the phrasing of the social theorist Anthony Giddens, people are knowledgeable agents in creating patterns across time and interacting with these configurations. We form our identities through how we participate in producing and reproducing social structures that can facilitate or place limits on our actions. Rather than giving priority to human agency or social structure, he asserts a mutually constituting arrangement, which he calls the duality of structure. Our actions create, maintain, and change the patterns that make our activities recognizable to others.[2] Special collections are one such place where activities extend across time and in which people act to produce and reproduce social relations, with effects that reverberate.

Special collections constitute systems that constrain or enable the (re)production of social structure, both inside and outside of their walls. We can see facets of the dialectic between donors and special collections in negotiations about how to select what is historical, over how to interpret objects, and regarding sources of authority in heritage activities. As a sphere for social action, special collections embody a double hermeneutic that Giddens predicts: the framework that heritage professionals create for understanding the meanings of objects over time comes to shape the legacy-seeking behaviors of the very people whose objects we must acquire in order to maintain cultural authority.

We are individuals acting within institutions, just as those who offer items for acquisition are actors within their own communities. As passionate advocates for heritage stewardship, we too are engaged in legacy-seeking behaviors. Special collections gain authority by adhering to professional standards and ensuring continuity, and they practice authenticity in stewarding materials most proximate to lived experience. At the same time, donors seek to align with or perhaps redirect the authority of a repository in order to better position and support their own worldviews and priorities. The donors and communities with whom we engage embed themselves within how we do our work, generate new possible trajectories, and with us cocreate a system of authority, authenticity, and cultural persistence.

We might apply structuration as the process by which systems produce meaning from historical materials through the interplay of known meanings, particularly of those who create and have created practices around an object, as well as the discovery (perhaps uncovering?) of new meanings in different contexts, quite apart from those in the past. Rather than being completely free of or impossibly bound by the past or present, individuals make choices about and engage in perpetuating, resculpting, overturning, and creating anew the social practices that become guidelines and resources for us. We create the stories that objects tell, in the way that we place ourselves at the center of interpretation, in how memory works, in the reflexive establishment of our identities through social praxis. We have a responsibility to keep doors open, even when we choose to not walk through them ourselves, considering that to cross a threshold may change what an object means, and acknowledging that entrances also comprise exits.

NOTES

1. Gabriel A. Radvansky, Andrea K. Tamplin, and Sabine A. Krawietz, "Walking through Doorways Causes Forgetting: Environmental Integration," *Psychonomic Bulletin and Review* 17, no. 6 (2010), 900–04.
2. Key works by Anthony Giddens include *Central Problems in Social Theory: Action, Structure, and Contradiction in Social Analysis* (Berkeley: University of California Press, 1979); *New Rules of Sociological Method: A Positive Critique of Interpretive Sociologies* (New York: Basic Books, 1976); *The Constitution of Society: Outline of the Theory of Structuration* (Berkeley: University of California Press, 1984); and *Modernity and Self-Identity: Self and Society in the Late Modern Age* (Stanford, CA: Stanford University Press, 1991).

CHAPTER 2

Affinities and Alliances

Thoughts on Acquisitions, Collection Development, and Donor Relations

JIM KUHN

The topic of this essay is collection acquisition—notably via gift—and the sort of collection policies, evolving tools, and best practices that can help guide our relationships with donors and our assessments of gifts-in-kind as we work to build collections that have research and pedagogical value for our increasingly diverse communities. Acquisition through gift is an issue of perennial importance for archives, rare book, and special collections departments; no less so at the University of Rochester, whose relationship with donors goes back to our mid-nineteenth-century founding. Our oldest printed book—a 1472 *Summa Theologiae* printed in Esslingen by Konrad Fyner—was one of our earliest gifts, from John Whipple Dwinelle, in 1859.

Gifts-in-Kind

Over the course of the last couple of years my collection development colleagues and I have had many grateful discussions with potential donors of gift-in-kind collections. Those that concluded with acquisitions included donor discussions about L. Frank Baum and H. G. Wells; about the corporate archive of an audiovisual consulting firm active from the 1960s through the early 1990s; about additional accruals to a collection of over 7,300 AIDS education posters; about an accrual of additional records from an independent nonprofit literary publisher, BOA Editions, Ltd., whose 178 boxes already with us have been fully processed and are on the cusp of public access, in time for the fortieth anniversary of the press in 2016.[1] This is a fairly short list; a fuller accounting of primarily unsolicited recent important donations would include the papers of a deceased local Episcopal bishop active in social justice circles; the work produced by a Rochester documentary filmmaking firm for Kodak in support of nationwide amateur photography communities, multiple archival collections from prominent retired faculty members, and a remarkable continuing stream of chromolithographed horticultural catalogs and publications issued by the very active nineteenth-century Rochester seed and nursery trade and donated by a former manuscript librarian.[2] Still not a complete list. Nor does this list include the many collections about which we have engaged in discussions, but respectfully—and gratefully—declined. I suspect this recent University of Rochester experience, that is, nearly constantly being in a position to acquire what one "Acknowledging the Past, Forging the Future" panelist described as collections that "come in over the transom unsolicited"—is not at all uncommon among special collections that actively acquire material through donation.[3]

Whether a collection on offer is acquired or not, these are all fascinating and important collections, and imbued with meanings different from those we might attribute as rare book and special collections librarians and archivists.[4] We are grateful for these discussions; all of us—collectors, donors, archivists, librarians, booksellers, auction houses—take seriously our shared and diverse commitments to preserving and providing access to cultural heritage. In those instances where the University of Rochester River Campus Libraries is not the right home for collections being offered, we readily make suggestions about alternatives, about planning for disposition, about what we can do to help. We are hardly alone in this practice, and these experiences should never be uncommon among special collections librarians and archivists. The question this essay addresses relates to new tools and best practices that could be helpful in successful collection building, particularly around gifts-in-kind, and perhaps especially around unsolicited gifts or those that do not necessarily build on existing institutional strengths.

Collection Development

Questions about when to say "yes" or "thank you no," arise in all offers of gifts-in-kind. What are the affinities between incoming and existing collections, the alliances that can be built between collectors and their collections with campus curricula, with faculty and graduate student research agendas, or among the campus library and local communities? A variety of tools and open practices can help in determining which answer—"yes" or "thank you no"—makes the most sense on a case-by-case basis. As our new collection development and management policy states, "we acknowledge and honor our crucial partnerships with friends and donors over the years; their interest and trust are one indication of the true worth of our endeavors."[5] Reaching a mutual understanding of collection development among archivists, curators, librarians, and donors can help strengthen these important relationships.

A publicly posted collection development policy for the River Campus Libraries Department of Rare Books, Special Collections, and Preservation went online in 2014. As a collection that dates back to the mid-nineteenth century, these holdings are large and varied.[6] This new policy therefore is a living document, tracking collection strengths we intend to build, the purpose of which is "not to document all collection strengths and areas of distinction, but to guide current selection criteria by designating certain areas of continued growth and indicating, where appropriate, collecting qualifiers and limited procedures for deaccessioning."[7]

However, in addition to listing a number of collecting areas of importance in rare books, children's books, literary, historical, university archives, and other manuscript and archival collections, the policy also notes both that

> The unique history of Rochester has meant that our collections contain substantial materials relating to often under-collected communities and cultures; we actively build on those existing holdings and seek opportunities to explore new areas. Through our collections, we facilitate study and research from multicultural and interdisciplinary perspectives.

And that

> This plan is not intended to be a final statement but will be reviewed at regular intervals and revised as required. In addition to subject areas documented here, we seek opportunities to acquire new collections that are of sufficient substance and depth to result in new areas of research strength.[8]

Our audiences and communities of use are increasingly diverse, both on and off campus. Generations of previous Rochester special collections staff and directors have helped build a collection that goes well beyond a traditional focus on documenting primarily European or mainstream white American cultural heritage. An individual and collective challenge in the profession remains how best to carry such practices into the future, and how to ensure that new areas of possible collecting are not neglected due, for instance, to implicit bias, or to important changes on campus or in our larger communities to which we may be slow to react.[9] What alliances might we miss if our mission is to build only on present strengths?

Policy statements are only effective as implemented.[10] And so bi-weekly collection development meetings are important venues for talking with colleagues about opportunities for purchase or for gift-in-kind, about connections with existing collections, and with current curricular strengths and activities, as are specific one-on-one conversations across campus with faculty members working in Science Fiction, Medieval Studies, Linguistics, and so on, about the potential usefulness of our collections for their teaching and research.[11] But additional useful practices exist that can help implement clear policy statements, and can inform discussions that come out of a commitment to open communication with potential donors.[12]

New Tools for Building Affinities and Alliances

At a time when more and more special collections departments are collecting born-digital materials, and most of us are well into our second decade digitizing analog materials; at a time when all archivally based research and teaching necessarily include deep digs into online textual or archival corpora as well as bibliographical databases; at a time when many university library budgets are flat or worse—at such a time special collections librarians and rare book curators are in need of updated tools for print and archival collection development. As Dupont and Yakel put this

> Special collections and archives can and do contribute unique value to research and learning, but their value has not been effectively communicated due to a lack of standards and best practices for measuring and assessing their impact. Although past efforts to define and operationalize special collections and archival metrics have not met with much success, the current focus of research libraries on value propositions and return on investment provides a new opportunity to remedy the deficiency.[13]

Although this essay is not concerned primarily with user-centered metrics and assessment techniques, a variety of additional, perhaps kindred, best practices might be advocated for, and are beginning to be considered at the River Campus Libraries.

Distinctive Print Collections

In an age of mass digitization, how can we best build and maintain distinctive print collections, as compared to EEBO, ECCO, Hathi, and NCCO?[14] Put differently, what would a checklist for comparing print copies in hand or on offer with the ubiquitous digital look like? Collating a specific print copy with an online copy is certainly possible with a portable optical collator (although my own eyes could use a bit more practice before I am confident at such hybrid collation).[15] But what about reasons to buy, or to accept a gift-in-kind? How should we articulate to administrators, or better yet to undergraduates, why specific physical copies are important—not despite the online access that is available but in fact *because* of that online access? When should rare book curators and others with purchasing authority buy physical copies when Hathi or ECCO availability exists on campus? When should print copies be retained despite new access to online "copies" through trusted digital repositories? "Always" is likely the answer on most of our lips at the moment, but is not likely to remain the answer in years to come.

Among projects that seem promising in addressing some of these questions is *Book Traces,* "a crowd-sourced web project aimed at identifying unique copies of nineteenth- and early twentieth-century books on library shelves," with a focus "on customizations made by original owners in personal copies, primarily in the form of marginalia and inserts."[16] Sponsored by NINES (Networked Infrastructure for Nineteenth-Century Electronic Scholarship) at the University of Virginia and led by NINES Director Andrew Stauffer, the project's focus on encouraging library-user identification of books showing history of readership is aimed in part to "help devise a triage process for discovering them, cataloging them more fully, and making better-informed decisions about print collections management."[17] With luck, unique copies of books from the machine-press era will be saved through such efforts; in addition, such consciousness-raising about the importance of readership traces in our open stacks should help spur new research into the unique aspects of open stack collections while encouraging both rare book and general collection catalogers to continue local enhancement of bibliographic records with copy-specific details.

One data-driven tool we have begun to put to use in evaluating both rare and open stack print collections is the GreenGlass service offered (until its recent acquisition by OCLC) by a company called Sustainable Collection Services.[18] Although most institutions have used the tool primarily to evaluate circulating collections, the River Campus Libraries chose to include rare printed holdings in our data set as well, with the result that we now have a collection visualization tool that provides data about our LC-classed printed holdings in both general and rare stacks, and how these compare broadly to other local, state, national, and online collections.

For instance, with GreenGlass data we can now evaluate which among our rare and open stacks printed items are

- in the public domain but not present in HathiTrust: i.e., probable local candidates for digitization and contribution to HathiTrust
- not held by Center for Research Libraries, that is, probable candidates for public commitment to print retention

- locally held but also full-text online via HathiTrust, regardless of copyright status, i.e., possible candidates for storage at our local offsite annex, after bibliographic record enhancement with copy-specific details

Although the marketing language for this service focuses on how to "responsibly drawdown" print collections, my colleagues and I contend that the tool can be used to help justify keeping print copies in our special collections and open stacks, that is, as we collectively begin to look closer at our collections, to compare them with the holdings of others, and to digital surrogates, we will discover far more unique copies than previously suspected, including those currently identified as duplicates.[19] The hope is that we may—through access to fuller comparative data about our holdings—begin to make better-informed decisions about digitization, about public commitment to print retention, about on-site retention, and about areas for possible metadata enhancement.

A further effort at encouraging enhanced "hybrid" access to both print and online holdings by special collections researchers includes our decision to test load certain HathiTrust bibliographic records into the River Campus Libraries' Voyager database.[20] This test is aimed at investigating the feasibility, cost, and usefulness of loading records for targeted subsets of HathiTrust public domain titles, aimed at specific classifications corresponding to rare book and special collections strengths in the River Campus Libraries and the George Eastman House International Museum of Photography and Film.[21] Specific proposed Library of Congress classification ranges to be included are SB1-SB1110 (Plant Culture) and TR (Photography). The hope here is that a modest and targeted integration of access to print, archival, and digitized online holdings through the Voyager catalog will enhance research and access experience for all users, but especially those with a primary research interest in areas of strength in our special collections.

Collaborations

Meanwhile, formal print retention partnerships are expanding, another promising development in helping libraries evaluate how individual institutional choices might affect the "collective collection." For instance, the University of Rochester is now a member of the Eastern Academic Scholars' Trust (EAST). Formerly known as the Northeast Regional Library Print Management Project, as of July 2014 this newly forming shared print retention partnership includes sixty libraries in New England, New York, and Pennsylvania and "will use a 'distributed retention model' whereby libraries become retention partners committed to retaining and sharing designated print copies of monographs and journals for use of the patrons of any of the libraries participating in EAST."[22] EAST-designated print retention copies must circulate, meaning that most of this work will go on in general stacks of member institutions; still, a fuller understanding of the regional distribution of print copies can only help inform local decisions about individual volumes, and their appropriate retention, circulation status, or designation for transfer into (or perhaps in some cases out of) rare and special collections stacks.

On a more local level, we work in the "burned over district" of Western New York, and the nineteenth century's Second Great Awakening.[23] Congregationalists, Baptists, Methodists, Latter Day Saints, Millerites, Shakers, Utopians, table-rapping Spiritualists; abolitionists, suffrage activists, temperance moralizers and social radicals—there are strong and deep research collections throughout central and western New York in all of these areas—as there are also in the history of photography. And this is just one example of a single region in a single state. Of course, strong regional, state, and national rare and special collections holdings exist and overlap across multiple institutions throughout the country. Regardless of an institution's location, a fuller knowledge by special collections librarians and archivists of local and regional holdings should influence decisions to purchase, or to accept via gift, collection material.

For instance, our collecting related to the life, career, and influence of George Eastman necessarily is influenced by the work of a local and internationally prominent museum and sister institution. For this reason, our posted policy indicates that

> Recognizing that there is overlap with the holdings and collecting practices of the George Eastman House International Museum of Photog-

raphy and Film, we actively acquire manuscript and book materials that directly relate to Eastman and his career through gift or purchase.[24]

We therefore typically discuss acquisitions through gift or purchase with the House, particularly when such potential acquisitions are of the type of material that might be among "hidden" or under-cataloged collections at each institution.

A bit further afield in Western New York are significant holdings in utopian societies at Syracuse University, which is the repository for the Oneida Community.[25] Therefore although our collecting policy states that "we selectively acquire manuscript and printed materials relating to the nineteenth-century Spiritualism movement, its proponents, opponents, and practitioners through gift or purchase," we do not actively seek to add holdings of utopian societies where such collecting may overlap with our neighboring institution.

Similarly, as we consider what collections might be added to support the research value of our growing collection of AIDS posters covering more than thirty years of a continuing epidemic, we are mindful of regional collections with related strengths. Our collection is strongest in AIDS posters, but we have additional and at present uncataloged collections of AIDS-related ephemera, books, and journals. Our collection will never—nor should it aspire to—duplicate the scope and holdings of the Cornell Human Sexuality Collection.[26] On the contrary, as we continue to add to our holdings on the global history of the AIDS epidemic and its response, we can better serve the human sexuality researcher in Western New York whose scope is more limited. And so, for instance, as the River Campus Libraries continue to work closely with the Archival and Historical Preservation Initiative of the Shoulders To Stand On program of the Gay Alliance of the Genesee Valley (GAGV) to build Rochester-related collections in this area, GAGV holdings themselves will continue to go to Cornell, which already holds the collection of record for this important local activist group.[27]

One final, anonymized, Western New York example will help prove the point: an approximately nine-and-one-half ton publisher's archive left Rochester-area storage in early 2015, bound not for collections at the University of Rochester, but for a peer institution in another state, after a successful round of collaboration by a number of special collections librarians in support of its intact preservation.

These sorts of collaborations have quietly been going on for generations, and will certainly continue. To what extent could open, formal, and publicly documented collaborative collection development help strengthen these efforts? I hope that new affinities and alliances are waiting to be built—not just of the traditional sort among special collections librarians and donors, booksellers, and auction-houses—but also between and among collecting institutions themselves. Through such strengthened inter-institutional ties we can begin collectively—and locally—to address bracing challenges such as those expressed by Yale University Librarian Susan Gibbons in her welcome and opening remarks to a 2013 conference, "Past Forward! Meeting Stakeholder Needs in Twenty-First Century Special Collections."

> It's one thing to say to the President, to the Provost, to Library Directors and others, about the collections that we already have... that we have a stewardship responsibility to take care of these... even though it is quite expensive to do so—the preservation, conservation, the environmental conditions, the space, all of that. But going forward as we bring in more collections, that's a harder one to argue.... For us to say it's important for us to bring in these new collections which will require in perpetuity more stewardship responsibilities when our budgets are shrinking and we have many other constraints.... The argument back will be "I agree someone has to take care of this collection but does it have to be our institution? Why *our* institution...?" We know what the answers are, but are we good at articulating this? Are we good at expressing this?[28]

Through use of open-policy publication, data-driven, and collaboration-oriented tools for building alliances, perhaps we can begin to increase our effectiveness at articulating the paths by which our collections should and will grow and strengthen. And in so doing we will have compelling new ways to engage in open communication with potential donors of gifts-in-kind.

Donor Relations

Traditional donor stewardship will of course continue to be a critically important part of our roles as stewards of archival, rare book, and special collections. I'll close with two collaborative alliances with major collectors in the completist vein, as examples of modest ways of extending the significance of their gifts—both of which, as it happens, are of poster collections.[29] These are the sort of collectors described by Geoffrey Smith at the "Acknowledging the Past, Forging the Future" colloquium as:

> the private collector who from a universe of knowledge has a passion, an intellectual design, and gathers together disparate parts of that and puts together in many cases with great passion strong wonderful collections that become monuments to scholarship.[30]

First, visitors to the Department of Rare Books, Special Collections and Preservation through December 22, 2014, had a rare opportunity to see one hundred years of posters recently donated from an important Gilbert and Sullivan collection largely still in private hands.[31] Bequeathed to the University in 2003, the Harold A. Kanthor Collection of Gilbert and Sullivan saw a 2004–2005 exhibition in the department from the privately held collection.[32] That collection has continued to grow for the past decade, and is now starting to come to us in outright annual gifts. Hence our recent remarkable exhibition of gifted posters, showing a wide variety of graphic designs, and depicting the production history of Gilbert and Sullivan operas and how they have been adapted, parodied, and translated into foreign languages. Dr. Kanthor has led tours of the exhibit; the Hopeman Memorial Carillon in Rush Rhees Library's tower performed a Gilbert and Sullivan concert for our 2014 homecoming weekend; and Dr. Kanthor has provided invaluable assistance in cataloging and inventorying the collection. This collaboration included a welcome donor stipulation for both public exhibition and poster cataloging as part of the agreement to donate. When is a bequest more than a bequest? When it also can act as a recurring gift, over time.

My final example is for visitors to the online projects website of our department, and an international, multilingual database of digitized

AIDS Education Posters now numbering over 7,300 (aep.lib.rochester.edu). Put together by Dr. Edward C. Atwater over the course of more than two decades, the physical posters were given starting in 2006, with additional accruals up through the present. Dating from 1982, and documenting efforts to educate and inform the people of over one hundred countries in over sixty languages, this collection is easiest to research in its online form. But there is no substitute for seeing the posters themselves—some of which are large multi-panel billboards. And so we frequently make use of the posters in teaching; in campus exhibits around December 1, World AIDS Day; and have reproduced a number of them on vinyl for use in traveling and outdoor exhibits.[33]

The donor's stipulation—with Rochester's enthusiastic agreement—that the posters be digitized and cataloged online has meant that as a continuing collector, Dr. Atwater can purchase additional posters without duplication. And this really is the best way to provide student and researcher access. However, although we own the posters, we do not own the copyrights. And so our site includes an online disclaimer and takedown notice, assembled with the cooperation of university counsel, which reads as follows:

> Copyright: The posters in the collection are presented here for research purposes only, and may be protected by copyright either according to US law or according to the laws applicable in their countries of origin. Any further reproduction of the materials may require copyright or other rights clearance and is the sole responsibility of the user.
>
> If you are the copyright holder for materials in this collection and would prefer that the image of the item(s) not appear on this website, please let us know. We hope that in making your decision, you will consider the place your work has in adding to a comprehensive understanding of the education effect that these posters were, and are, a part of.[34]

I should add that in the seven years since the website launch, the River Campus Libraries have never received a takedown request. One "Acknowledging the Past, Forging the Future" participant challenged us to consider how we might engage in collaborative transformative non-infringing uses of our collections, in keeping with principles of fair use.[35] I think of this—and other—AIDS Poster Collections as providing a model approach.[36]

Conclusion

Publicly posted collection development policies that don't rely solely on building on existing strengths, along with open communication and a data-driven approach to collaboration and alliance-building, can help us extend and enhance access to our unique collections while helping to guide our choices in collection building through donation. Our policies should balance collaboration with the private collector and his or her "monument to scholarship" with new consideration for how our collections should grow in affinities and alliances with neighbor institutions, with the underrepresented local communities perhaps currently beyond our ken; but also, and perhaps increasingly, should address the continuing question that we each individually, and together collectively, confront: "Why *our* institution?"

NOTES

1. The David Perlman Oz Collection is now fully cataloged; portions were exhibited in the 2014 on-site exhibition "'Acquiring Minds': Building Special Collections, 2009–2014." Lyman Frank Baum had a local connection; he performed under the stage name of Louis F. Baum in a February 1883 Rochester production of his own play *The Maid of Arran*. The Andrew Hunt Gordon Collection of H. G. Wells, given by an alum ('70, MS Geology) is being processed into the collections at the time of this writing. The corporate archive Hope Reports Collection is accompanied by a full run of the publications issued by Thomas W. Hope (1969–2000). The AIDS Education Posters Collection, online at https://aep.lib.rochester.edu, is discussed in greater detail in the last section of this paper.
2. The department includes quite a few collections documenting Rochester's strong social reform and social justice movements. Our nineteenth-century collections in this area have a strong focus on abolitionism and women's rights. Our twentieth-century local history collections continue this trend, but expand into other areas as well, for instance, politics (e.g., Rochester Socialist Scrapbook Collection, 1910–1919, Call number: D.110); the events and aftermath of the 1964 Rochester riots (e.g., among others, the P. David Finks Papers, 1965–2009, Call number: D.393); the Franklin Florence Papers, 1962–1972, Call number: D.167; the Rochester Race Riot Papers,

1964–1966, Call number: D.185); and the local history of gay rights (e.g., a full run and online public access to Rochester's *The Empty Closet,* one of the oldest continuously published LGBT papers in the United States). The River Campus Libraries houses corporate and research laboratory archives for the Eastman Kodak Company, the largest of which is our Kodak Historical Collection #003, 1854–2006, Call number: D.319. The department also houses the University Archives, which selectively adds the papers of retiring faculty, staff, and alumni with relevance to the University and its institutional history. And the department holds the collection of record, including the corporate research library, of the Ellwanger and Barry Company of Rochester, as well as other firms who helped make the city a horticultural capital during the latter half of the nineteenth century. For more on these collections, see the numerous articles published on Ellwanger and Barry and other nursery firms and on chromolithographed horticultural plates, in the *University of Rochester Library Bulletin,* as well as Blake McKelvey, "The Flower City," *Rochester Historical Society Publications* 18 (1940), 121–69.
3. Geoffrey Smith, Selby Kiffer, Jon Lindseth, Jim Kuhn, and Christoph Irmscher, "Where Are We Today?" a panel discussion presented at "Acknowledging the Past, Forging the Future" (Cleveland, OH, October 22, 2014): 19:06, https://youtu.be/FkNA2XAx5yA.
4. A variety of essays address the multivariate ways in which archival materials have meanings that may be incommensurable with, potentially inscribed over, or otherwise elided by well-meaning traditional archival practices. Among the essays that have helped address such issues in considering the past and future work of a department that includes both nineteenth- and twentieth-century social justice movements include Andrew Flinn, "Other Ways of Thinking, Other Ways of Being," in *What Are Archives?* ed. L. Craven (Aldershot: Ashgate, 2008), 109–28; Randall C. Jimerson, "Archives for All," *American Archivist* 70 (2007): 252–81; Annemaree Lloyd, "Guarding Against Collective Amnesia?," *Library Trends* 56 (2007): 53–65; Joan M. Schwartz and Terry Cook, "Archives, Records, and Power," *Archival Science* 2 (2002): 1–19.
5. University of Rochester River Campus Libraries Department of Rare Books, Special Collections and Preservation, "Collection Development and Management," www.library.rochester.edu/rbscp/collectiondevelopment.
6. Collection overviews, guides, and statements of strengths can be found in a number of past publications. For instance, the departmental website subject guides are based in large part on University of Rochester Library, *Guide to the Collections* (Rochester, NY: The Library, 1994). Other descriptions, including annual lists of gifts, can be found in back issues of the *University of Rochester Library Bulletin.* See, for example, "Our Special Collections," IV (1949): 45–55, and "The Department of Special Collections: A Survey," XXIV (1968): 5–15.
7. University of Rochester River Campus Libraries Department of Rare Books, Special Collections and Preservation, "Collection Development and Management," www.library.rochester.edu/rbscp/collectiondevelopment.
8. Ibid.

9. One panel presentation at "Acknowledging the Past, Forging the Future" was given by E. Haven Hawley (Chair, Special and Area Studies Collections Department, George A. Smathers Libraries, University of Florida). Dr. Hawley addressed collecting for marginalized or underrepresented communities, in an interrogation of traditional collecting practices through the lens of the Structuration theories of Anthony Giddens; see Joel Silver, Ken Lopez, Paul Ruxin, Daniel De Simone, and E. Haven Hawley, "Acknowledging the Past," a panel discussion presented at "Acknowledging the Past, Forging the Future" (October 21, 2014): 41:09–55:15, https://youtu.be/k6vYBWFdSw8. For essays that address these issues for an area of increasing interest at the River Campus Libraries, the LGBT and Queer collection material especially related to AIDS and sexual health, see Anna Conlan, "Representing Possibility," in *Gender, Sexuality and Museums,* ed. A. Levin (London: Routledge, 2010): 253–63; and Angela L. DiVeglia, "Accessibility, Accountability, and Activism," in *Make Your Own History,* ed. L. Bly and K. Wooten (Los Angeles: Litwin Books, 2012): 69–88.

10. A variety of recent documents proved useful in updating our collection development practices, including the work of Melissa Hubbard (Team Leader, Scholarly Resources and Special Collections), especially in the collection development diversity statement of the Kelvin Smith Library Scholarly Resources and Special Collections Collection Development Policy; a UK policy statement regarding "core collections which would not normally be considered for disposal" in Chartered Institute for Library and Information Professionals, "Disposals Policy for Rare Books and Manuscripts," www.cilip.org.uk/rare-books-and-special-collections-group/policy-statements/disposals-policy-rare-books-and; Steven K. Galbraith and Geoffrey D. Smith, "Getting to Know Your Collections," *Rare Book Librarianship* (Santa Barbara: Libraries Unlimited, 2012); and Society of American Archivists Technical Subcommittee on Guidelines for Reappraisal and Deaccessioning, *Guidelines for Reappraisal and Deaccessioning* (2012).

11. These expansive conversations at our institution do not—yet—approach the admirable goal described by Jay Satterfield (Special Collections Librarian, Dartmouth College) of "taking advice broadly" about potential acquisitions, where routing slips for catalogs include anyone in the Rauner Special Collections Library who is interested in seeing them, and where interns have successfully advocated for collection additions; see Jay Satterfield, "Considering the Present: Special Collections Are the Meal, Not the Dessert," presented at "Acknowledging the Past, Forging the Future" (October 21, 2014): 8:06, https://youtu.be/mlWonr6CY2M.

12. Updated formal gift-in-kind processing forms developed in consultation with advancement officers on campus, standardized deed of gift forms, and standard estimates for costs of processing and rehousing have proved useful traditional methods for building and documenting new relationships with donors of collection material. Our own recently updated forms are in large part based on guidance from Association of Research Libraries, "Model Deed of Gift, Including Mixed IP Rights," *Research Library Issues* 279 (2012): 7–9. Annual meetings of the Academic Library Advancement and Development Network, founded in 1996, have also proved to be

useful opportunities for networking with and learning from fundraising professionals, special collection librarians, and deans.

13. Christian Dupont and Elizabeth Yakel, "'What's So Special about Special Collections?' Or, Assessing the Value Special Collections Bring to Academic Libraries," *Evidence Based Library and Information Practice* 8 (2013): 9–21.

14. Chadwyck-Healey Early English Books Online, "Early English Books Online (EEBO)," http://eebo.chadwyck.com/home; Early English Books Online Text Creation Partnership, "Early English Books Online-Text Creation Partnership (EEBO-TCP)," www.textcreationpartnership.org/tcp-eebo/; Gale Cengage Learning, "Eighteenth Century Collections Online (ECCO)," http://gale.cengage.co.uk/product-highlights/history/eighteenth-century-collections-online.aspx; "HathiTrust Digital Library," https://www.hathitrust.org/; University of Rochester River Campus Libraries, "University of Rochester Libraries Join HathiTrust," www.library.rochester.edu/news/libraries-join-hathitrust; Gale Cengage Learning, "Nineteenth Century Collections Online (NCCO)," http://gale.cengage.co.uk/product-highlights/history/nineteenth-century-collections-online.aspx.

15. Optical collation has a history dating back at least to the Victorian period; see, for instance Daniel Zalewski, "Field Notes: Through the Looking Glass," *Lingua Franca* 7 (1997). For a sampling of recent work on experimental prototypes and techniques for optical and computer-aided textual collation, see Barbara Bordalejo, "Caxton's Editing of the Canterbury Tales," *Papers of the Bibliographical Society of America* 108 (2014): 41–60; Jim Kuhn, "'A Hawk from a Handsaw,'" in *New Technologies and Renaissance Studies II*, ed. T. Gniady, K. McAbee, and J. Murphy (Toronto: Iter, 2014): 67–90; *The Sapheos Project* (Columbia, SC: University of South Carolina, 2011); Judith Siefring and Pip Willcox, "More than Was Dreamt of in Our Philosophy," in *Digitizing Medieval and Early Modern Material Culture*, ed. B. Nelson and M. Terras (Tempe, AZ: Iter, 2012): 83–111; Pip Willcox, "'A Creature Native and Indued /Unto That Element'? Digitizing Hamlet: How to Start; Where to Stop," paper presented at *SDH 2011* (Copenhagen, November 17, 2011).

16. "Book Traces: About," www.booktraces.org/about/.

17. Ibid.

18. OCLC, "Sustainable Collection Services," https://www.oclc.org/sustainable-collections/features.en.html.

19. OCLC, "Sustainable Collection Services and GreenGlass," www.oclc.org/sustainable-collections.en.html.

20. Details about this and other options and features available to partner institutions are described online; see: HathiTrust, "HathiTrust Digital Library: Our Partnership," https://www.hathitrust.org/partnership.

21. The University of Rochester's Voyager catalog includes bibliographic records for a wider community than the River Campus Libraries. Also included are the print holdings of the George Eastman House, the University's Memorial Art Gallery, and the libraries—including special collections—of the University's School of Medicine and Dentistry (the Edward G. Miner Library and its Rare Books and Manuscripts

Section), and the Eastman School of Music (the Sibley Music Library, and its Ruth T. Watanabe Special Collections). This combined catalog facilitates local researcher access to holdings that are otherwise separately housed and administered.
22. Eastern Academic Scholars' Trust (EAST), "About Us," https://www.blc.org/east-project.
23. The appellation has its origin in Reverend Finney's 1876 Memoirs, which refers to western New York as a "burnt district;" see Charles G. Finney, *Memoirs of Rev. Charles G. Finney* (New York: Fleming H. Revell Co., 1876): 78. Whitney Cross wrote the classic twentieth-century account of this region's social, religious, and intellectual history; see Whitney R. Cross, *The Burned-Over District* (Ithaca, NY: Cornell University Press, 1950). The influence of Cross's landmark work on later historians is discussed usefully in a 1989 review; see Judith Wellman, "Crossing Over Cross," *Reviews in American History* 17 (1989): 159–74.
24. University of Rochester River Campus Libraries Department of Rare Books, Special Collections and Preservation, "Collection Development and Management," www.library.rochester.edu/rbscp/collectiondevelopment.
25. Syracuse University Libraries Special Collections Research Center, "Oneida Community Collection," http://library.syr.edu/find/scrc/collections/diglib/oneida/.
26. Cornell University Library Division of Rare and Manuscript Collections, "Human Sexuality Collection," http://rmc.library.cornell.edu/HSC/.
27. Evelyn Bailey, "Gay Alliance Places Historical Records in Permanent Repositories," *Shoulders to Stand On*, June 12, 2012, http://womenwopinions.typepad.com/shoulders_to_stand_on/2012/06/gay-alliance-places-historical-records-in-permanent-repositories.html; Cornell University Library Division of Rare and Manuscript Collections, "Guide to the Gay Alliance of the Genesee Valley Records, 1970–2012. Collection Number: 7560," http://rmc.library.cornell.edu/EAD/htmldocs/RMM07560.html.
28. Susan Gibbons, "Welcome and Opening Remarks," presented at "Past Forward! Meeting Stakeholder Needs in Twenty-First Century Special Collections," (New Haven, CT, June 4, 2013): 1:57, https://youtu.be/qFFRgTTv38M.
29. Collecting, preserving, and digitizing posters in special collections can present challenges unique to their format and content. Some useful perspectives on these challenges can be found in essays by Teetaert and Tschabrun; see Vince Teetaert, "Whatcha Doin' After the Demo?" in *Informed Agitation*, ed. M. Morrone (Sacramento, CA: Library Juice Press, 2014): 163–72; and Susan Tschabrun, "Off the Wall and into a Drawer," *American Archivist* 66 (2003): 303–24.
30. Geoffrey Smith, Selby Kiffer, Jon Lindseth, Jim Kuhn, and Christoph Irmscher, "Where Are We Today?," a panel discussion presented at "Acknowledging the Past" (October 22, 2014): 0:28, https://youtu.be/FkNA2XAx5yA.
31. Those unable to attend had an opportunity to see reproductions of a few of the posters in the alumni magazine; see Adam Fenster, "The Very Model of a Major Collection," *Rochester Review* 77 (2015): 8–9. Other major US Gilbert and Sullivan collections have long existed and been periodically exhibited at Harvard University

and the Morgan Library & Museum; the University of Rochester bequest is one of the few major US. collections still in private hands. In 2014 George Mason University received the David and Annabelle Stone Gilbert and Sullivan Collection, while in 2015, OSU Libraries' Jerome Lawrence and Robert E. Lee Theatre Research Institute received the Jesse and Rochelle Shereff Gilbert and Sullivan Collection; see Corey Jenkins Schaut, "Gilbert and Sullivan Collection to Make Its Home at Mason," *George Mason University News,* October 7, 2014, http://newsdesk.gmu.edu/2014/10/gilbert-sullivan-collection-make-home-mason/; Karla Strieb, "From the Director," *The Ohio State University—University Libraries—Libraries News and Information,* July 20, 2015, https://library.osu.edu/blogs/osulstaff/2015/07/20/from-the-director-july-20-2015-ala-technical-servicescollections-report/.

32. Harold Kanthor and the University of Rochester River Campus Libraries Department of Rare Books, Special Collections and Preservation, *Gilbert and Sullivan, From London to America* (Rochester, NY: University of Rochester, 2004).

33. For additional background about this collection, see Sarah Clune, "An Illustrated History of AIDS," *PBS Newshour,* December 1, 2011, www.pbs.org/newshour/rundown/an-illustrated-history-of-aids/; Hans Villarica, "From Haring to Condom Man: Art as Weapon in the War Against AIDS," *The Atlantic,* December 5, 2011, www.theatlantic.com/entertainment/archive/2011/12/from-haring-to-condom-man-art-as-weapon-in-the-war-against-aids/249229/. The literature on AIDS and art is vast. Selected resources for learning more specifically about the international history of AIDS educational and activist posters include, for instance, Centre Régional d'Information et de Prévention du SIDA, *Images and SIDA* (Paris: CRIPS, 1992–1996); Douglas Crimp and Adam Rolston, *AIDS Demo Graphics* (Seattle: Bay Press, 1990); Ted Gott, "Where the Streets Have New Aims," in *Don't Leave Me This Way* (Canberra: National Gallery of Australia, 1994): 187–211; Lutz Hieber and ACT UP, *Bilderschock* (Hannover: Bürgerinitiative Raschplatz e. V., 1990); Richard Meyer, "This Is to Enrage You," in *But Is It Art?* ed. N. Felshin (Seattle: Bay Press, 1995): 51–84; Hugh Rigby and Susan Leibtag, *HardWear* (Edmonton: Quon Editions, 1994); Tommaso Speratta, *Rebels Rebels* (Gent: Merz, 2014). To learn more about metadata- and copyright-related issues associated with collecting and providing meaningful access to the history of educational engagement with communities of gender and sexual diversity see, for instance, Emily Drabinski, "Teaching Other Tongues," *Journal of Information Ethics* 20 (2011): 42–55; K. J. Rawson, "Accessing Transgender // Desiring Queer(er?) Archival Logics," *Archivaria* 68 (2009): 123–40; K. R. Roberto, "Inflexible Bodies," *Journal of Information Ethics* 20 (2011): 56–64; Graham Willett and Steve Wright, "Copyright, Copywrong, and Ethics," in *Queers Online,* ed. R. Wexelbaum (Sacramento, CA: Litwin Books, 2015): 129–44. To learn about, as well as to find tools for dealing with censorship challenges that may arise in this context, see for instance: Marcel Barriault, "Hard to Dismiss," *Archivaria* 68 (2009): 219–46; James LaRue, "Responding to a Challenge," in *Serving LGBTIQ Library and Archives Users,* ed. by E. Greenblatt (Jefferson: McFarland, 2010): 278–81; William Leonard and Anne Mitchell, "The

Use of Sexually Explicit Materials in HIV/AIDS Initiatives Targeted at Gay Men," Australian National Council, 2000; Svetlana Mintcheva, "Art Censorship Today," in *Library Juice Press Handbook of Intellectual Freedom,* ed. by M. Alfino and L. Koltutsky (Sacramento: Library Juice Press, 2014): 334–62; Rachel Wexelbaum, "Censorship of Online LGBTIQ Content in Libraries," in *Queers Online,* ed. by R. Wexelbaum (Sacramento, CA: Litwin Books, 2015): 205–13.

34. University of Rochester River Campus Libraries Department of Rare Books, Special Collections and Preservation, "AIDS Education Posters Collection: About," http://aep.lib.rochester.edu/about.

35. Alice Schreyer, "Exploring the Past," presented at "Acknowledging the Past, Forging the Future" (Cleveland, OH, October 21, 2014), https://youtu.be/XD7hwqstRhI.

36. Inviting out-outs or take-down notices is becoming more common in special collections departments. At the University of Rochester we are in fact indebted to the UCLA Louise M. Darling Biomedical Library History and Special Collections Division, whose opt-out procedure for its own online AIDS Poster site was the inspiration for the River Campus Libraries' approach; see University of California, Los Angeles Louise M. Darling Biomedical Library History and Special Collections Division, "AIDS Posters: Copyright and Opt-Out Procedure," http://digital.library.ucla.edu/aidsposters/optout.html. It is fitting then that this essay close with a sincere thanks and acknowledgment to the work of UCLA special collection colleagues, and indeed all of those whose efforts have helped to shape, to inform, and to mentor "Where We Are Today." A previous version of this paper was presented at "Acknowledging the Past, Forging the Future," (held October 21–22, 2014, at Case Western Reserve University's Kelvin Smith Library,), as part of the "Where Are We Today?," a panel discussion moderated by Geoffrey Smith (Head of the Rare Books and Manuscripts Library, The Ohio State University), and including Selby Kiffer (Senior Vice President, Sotheby's), Jon Lindseth (Private Collector), and Christoph Irmscher (Provost Professor, George F. Getz Jr. Professor in the Wells Scholars Program, Wells Scholars Program Director, Indiana University Bloomington). My thanks to Melissa Hubbard and her colleagues for organizing this conference and for helpful comments on earlier drafts of this paper, and to the panel moderator and participants for a lively and wide-ranging discussion.

# CHAPTER 3

Where Does the Collector/Donor Community See Special Collections Today?

JON A. LINDSETH

I am a bibliophile, a book collector, and donor to library special collections.

Terry Belanger, the founder of Rare Book School at the University of Virginia, has said that book collectors like nothing better than talking about their collections, and their friends like nothing worse than having to listen.

Joel Silver, director of the Lilly Library at Indiana, wrote, "have you ever tried to explain book collecting to someone who is not a collector? This has never been an easy thing to do."[1]

"Where are we today?" is a question about the status of special collections. The answer is that the libraries I am affiliated with—the Cornell University Library, the Morgan Library & Museum, and the British Library—are all in pretty good shape, even if they are constrained principally by money. Money often limits everything at libraries and their special collections because acquisitions occur by purchase, donation, or a combination of the two. Even if collections are donated, they require space and catalogers' time to process, two other commodities that are also in short supply.

Because library special collections material often comes from either collectors or from the archives of writers, what should special collections librarians do to identify potential donors and to encourage them to see that their library is well-suited as the donor's choice?

Part I: Communities

The Harry Ransom Center at The University of Texas has made an art of identifying writers, seeking out and befriending them, and making its library the first choice for purchase or gift. However, with material now created and revised electronically, the future of these archival sources will be significantly reduced. Harry Ransom had a plan. He believed, correctly, that to have a great university, a great library was a necessity. Before Ransom The University of Texas lacked one, but not now, and it continues to acquire archives and collections because it still follows the plan.

Libraries have many needs and scarce financial resources, while collectors can narrowly target their resources. We can collect over a long time period in sometimes arcane and narrow fields, collecting in great depth, and adding tangential and ephemeral items to flesh out a collection.

If my premise is correct, it is often collectors who provide the raw material that feeds and grows library special collections, and thereby assure the future success of libraries to meet the needs of scholars. What should the plan of the curators be to identify, to get to know, and to nurture these collectors? A quote that I first heard from Marty Marshall, a professor of marketing at the Harvard Business School is that "if your plans aren't in writing you don't have plans." How many of today's library special collections have up-to-date written plans? How many of your plans target specific material, and most importantly, the potential collectors who own relevant material? What are you doing every day to nurture these collectors, and to sell them on your library as a potential repository? Some wags say that "selling is like shaving. If you don't do it every day, you're a bum!"[2]

The past and the future of special collections depends in part upon generous donations of book collectors. Who are these collectors? A great deal has been written about book collectors over the years, and it's not all good.

It is said that George Bernard Shaw once remarked that collectors never read anything. The Nobel Prize winner in literature, Orhan Pamuk of Turkey, confirmed this. He is quoted as saying "I would not really describe myself as a collector. I do have 16,000 books, but I have read them all." (That works out to 320 books per year, each year for 50 years.) He went on, "a collector would be someone with 20,000 books who has never so much as opened one. Collecting is about owning; it is a compensation for something else."³

The writer Robertson Davies wrote in 1951 that collectors and book lovers are people who enjoy their books "more often in thought than in reality."⁴

In 1899, the English Latinist and poet A. E. Housman, said of the Cleveland Rowfant Club member Paul Lamperly, that "I think yours is the only letter containing no nonsense that I have ever received from a stranger."⁵ Housman later wrote that book collectors are an "idiotic class," a view likely held by some collectors' spouses.⁶

The late collector and real estate developer, Albert H. Small, whose two vast collections are at the University Virginia and George Washington University, is credited with having said, "When you are bitten, collecting is a disease that is hard to cure."⁷

The bibliophile Thomas Frognall Dibdin titled his 1809 book *The Bibliomania: Or, Book-Madness; Containing Some Account of the History, Symptoms, and Cure of This Fatal Disease*.⁸

Nicholas Basbanes titled his 1995 book about book collectors simply: *A Gentle Madness*.⁹

Collecting often gets confused with accumulating. The British journal *The Book Collector*, founded by Ian Fleming, reviewed a book titled *Stuff: Compulsive Hoarding and the Meaning of Things*. The review states "*Stuff* is not primarily concerned with book hoarders, but no book collector can fail to be struck by the analogous compulsion that these poor sufferers exhibit. It is not a stretch to see the same paraphilia in the collector who is obsessive about *Alice in Wonderland* or printed ephemera or air dropped leaflets or nudie postcards, is it?"¹⁰ The writer is hitting close to home here, as I am an *Alice's Adventures in Wonderland* collector.

When Alice met the Cheshire Cat in Wonderland, he said to her: "I'm mad, you're mad. We're all mad here." She asked how he knew she was mad, and he responded simply: "You must be or you wouldn't have come here." So fair warning, everyone.

The California accountant and book collector William Barlow spoke in 1983 at The Library of Congress. He titled his talk "Book Collecting: Personal Rewards and Public Benefits."¹¹ Personal rewards come to collectors in the knowledge we gain, and in seeing our collections taking shape and being used, and in the friends we make. One important public benefit comes when our collections go to libraries for both preservation and for use by students and scholars.

The late D. F. McKenzie, Professor of Bibliography and Textual Criticism at Oxford, wrote "the book, in all its forms, enters history only as evidence of human behavior and it remains active only in the service of human needs."[12]

Special collections are needed and will continue to be, and collectors have and will continue to be essential partners to ensure the continued success of special collections.

NOTES

1. Joel Silver, "It's a Book—Not an App," *Fine Books and Collections* (Summer 2012), www.finebooksmagazine.com/issue/1003/physical-books-1.phtml.
2. This quote has been attributed to a number of people. Perhaps the more reliable attribution is to Alex Stanley Kroll, a football player and advertising agency executive, as found at www.quotes.net/quote/14926 and at http://izquotes.com/quote/330116. A different attribution is to Jack Schwartz, a leader in the telephone sales industry, as found in Gary Goodman, "Cold Calling Is Like Shaving—If You Don't Do It Every Day You're a Bum," *NBIZ Magazine* (Fall 2007), https://www.nbizmag.com/magarticles/coldcallingislikeshaving.pdf.
3. "Interview with Orhan Pamuk: 'The Museum of Innocence'—A Declaration of Love to the City of Istanbul." *Qantara.de*, November 5, 2012, https://en.qantara.de/content/interview-with-orhan-pamuk-the-museum-of-innocence-a-declaration-of-love-to-the-city-of. In a different interview that appeared a few days later, Pamuk's comment was phrased somewhat differently: "I'm not an obsessive collector. I perhaps have 16,000 books and wouldn't mind if one was stolen. A collector is a person who has 16,000 books and he is proud to have not read any of them. I'm not like that—I use them and read them," as quoted in Sameer Rahim. "Orhan Pamuk: A Book is a Promise," *The Telegraph,* November 9, 2012, www.telegraph.co.uk/culture/books/bookreviews/9663819/Orhan-Pamuk-A-book-is-a-promise.html.
4. Robertson Davies, *Tempest-Tost* (New York: Penguin, 1951). The full quote appears on a number of sites, including http://blog.gaiam.com/quotes/authors/robertson-davies/31513 or http://quoteseverlasting.com/author.php?a=Robertson%20Davies.
5. The quote is found in a letter from A. E. Housman to Paul Lamperly, Bryn Mawr College Library Special Collections. Collection Number: M57A.E. Housman Papers, 1859–1936. Part II: Box and Folder List- Outgoing Correspondence. Box 2, Folder 5.

6. Housman's reference to bibliophiles being an "idiotic class" was made in October 1922 in a letter to his publisher, Grant Richards, in response to a printing error of his *Last Poems*. According to the Antiquarian Booksellers' Association of America site, "Housman was fastidious about punctuation & was annoyed by the omission of punctuation marks in the first two lines of the poem on p. 52." Housman wrote in reply to Richards's suggestion that they could insert an errata slip in the remaining copies, "No, don't put in an errata slip. The blunder will probably enhance the value of the 1st edition in the eyes of bibliophiles, an idiotic class." The quote appears in *The Letters of A.E. Housman,* ed. Archie Burnett (Oxford: Oxford University Press, 2007), 515. This volume attributes the letter to Lilly MSS 1.1:.p.c. addressed "Grant Richards Esq. | 8 St. Martin's Street | Leicester Square | W. C. 2" Richards, 202; Maas, 204. See also www.abaa.org/book/249304967.
7. Variations on this quote have been made by many others, including Christopher Forbes, the son of Malcolm Forbes, who said in 2011 that "collecting is a disease, an affliction I inherited from my father. The symptoms are different for everyone, but the common denominator is that you can't help it." In Suzanne Gannon, "The Great Loves of Christopher Forbes," *Heritage Magazine* (Winter 2011): 41.
8. Thomas Frognall Dibdin, *Bibliomania; a Bibliographical Romance,* originally published in 1809 (London: Printed for Longman, Hurst, Rees, and Orme, Paternoster Row, 1809), with a revision in 1811 (London: Henry G. Bohn, 1811), which according to Wikipedia is a different work. "The 1809 Bibliomania is a slim mock treatise of about eighty pages purporting to diagnose and to cure the 'book-disease' (even as it gives every evidence of having succumbed to the disease itself), so that it fits into the genre of literary satire. The 1811 Bibliomania, on the other hand, has not only swelled to almost 800 pages, but has turned into a peculiar generic hybrid Dibdin terms 'bibliographical romance'." *Bibliomania; or Book Madness; A Bibliographical Romance, in Six Parts* (1811) "consists of dialogues on books and book-collecting conducted by a set of male characters (many based on Dibdin's actual friends), two of whom court shadowy female figures in the intervals between their more intense romancing of books," https://en.wikipedia.org/wiki/Bibliomania_(book).
9. Nicholas A. Basbanes, *A Gentle Madness: Bibliophiles, Bibliomanes, and the Eternal Passion for Books* (New York: H. Holt and Co., 1995).
10. Bruce Whiteman, "Review of *Stuff: Compulsive Hoarding and the Meaning of Things,* by Randy O. Frost and Gail Steketee," *The Book Collector* (Autumn 2011), 483.
11. William P. Barlow, Jr., *Book Collecting, Personal Rewards and Public Benefits: A Lecture Delivered at the Library of Congress on December 7, 1983* (Washington, DC: The Library, 1984).
12. Paul Eggert, "Brought to Book," *The Library* 13, no. 1 (March 2012): 3.

CHAPTER 4

Collecting Communities

The Role of Special Collections Librarians and Archivists in Creating New Life for Community-Based Collections

MELISSA A. HUBBARD

The future of special collection is community. This is hardly an original idea. There is an incredibly rich and increasingly active professional discourse about community-based collections that suggests that these kinds of collections are moving closer to the core of our work as special collections librarians and archivists. To advance in this direction, we should consider the potential role of special collections in building, documenting, and creating communities, and some of the changes that our professional community may undergo as we incorporate more of these collections into our work.

The Association of Research Libraries (ARL) recently defined community-based collections as those "that have been amassed not by one individual but by a collective, which may take the form of a museum, ethnic or cultural organization, or other diaspora group active in the documentation of its past."[1] It is this active community interest in documentation that separates these collections from institutional records and other archival collections that accrue records through internal processes. I would add to the ARL definition that community-based collections are built to support the needs and interests of their founding communities. They are generally not intended to support academic research and teaching, differentiating them from other artificial collections created by research libraries.

The Role and Importance of Community-Based Collections

Where do community-based collections fit within the history of the organizational constructions commonly known as special collections departments? In "The Evolution of the Concept of Special Collections in American Research Libraries," William L. Joyce traces the history of special collections by tying the development of collections to trajectories in the research agendas of American university faculty.[2] Since the 1980s, we've seen a shift in the literature about the nature of special collections, with many professionals advocating for a model of the special collections library focused on education and outreach rather than research. Articles such as "From 'Treasure Room' to 'School Room': Special Collections and Education" by Steven Escar Smith argue for dramatically expanding the audience for special collections by prioritizing education at least as highly as research.[3] In his contribution to this book, Jay Satterfield makes a compelling case for situating special collections at the center of university curricula, and changing curatorial practices to support that model (see chapter 14). This emphasis on outreach and access also is extended in John Overholt's recent "Five Theses on the Future of Special Collections," in which he argues that special collections librarians will increasingly prioritize providing broad open access to collections in response to changes in the information technology environment.[4] Users are now accustomed to finding information online, and we must ensure that special collections can be accessed virtually if they are to remain relevant.

Special collections are most valuable when they are used. The role of the special collections librarian is to select materials that will likely receive significant usage by researchers, teachers, or students, and to provide ready access to the selected materials. Unfortunately, too often many items in special collections are divorced from their original context. The selected works may have been produced by a particular community long ago or far away (or both), and they now stand as the material remaining evidence of their communities. Through teaching and research, new contexts may be created for them as users investigate the items and use them to construct new narratives about their own history and culture. Special collections are often built from items selected from the antiquarian book marketplace, which comprises a community of dealers, collectors, and librarians. All members of this community have expertise in overlapping areas of information history and cultural heritage, and the materials they add to this marketplace are carefully selected for their expected value within this context.

Community-based collections are different from the types of collections described above in that they often retain a strong connection to the context of their original creation, even when they are acquired by research institutions. When a community creates a collection, it is still invested in its stewardship, and its members are the primary users of the collection. Items in community-based collections may never have circulated in the cultural heritage marketplace, but instead were selected and preserved by members of that community because of their value to a specific set of individuals. These individuals usually don't acquire or create items based on their perceived historical value for researchers and teachers who are outside of their immediate community, but rather because the items are important to the immediate needs of the community itself. When research institutions acquire these kinds of collections from the originating community, they must successfully address the continuing needs of said community, while also providing access to the collection in ways that support the research and teaching needs of their institutions. For community-based collections, librarians and archivists take on a new role in which they build relationships between and among the items in the collection, the community that created it, and researchers and teachers who would use the collection for new purposes. As we do this, our collections become platforms for active engagement with history and culture.

Community-Based Collections: The Cleveland Play House Archives—A Case Study

At Case Western Reserve University (CWRU), the Cleveland Play House (CPH) archives are an example of a community-based collection. Gifted to the library in 2012, it was founded as a community-based collection and it still meets community needs, though it is now more of an institutional archive. CPH was founded in 1915 by a small group of artists and theater-lovers who wanted to perform plays using modern European aesthetics. Although it now is recognized as the oldest regional theater in the United States, the founders probably could not have imagined what the Play House would become by 2015. Today it is a highly active and successful organization with almost one hundred people on staff, and its archives are one of the best collections in the country documenting the history of American theater.

Several of the women who were involved in founding CPH itself started the archives, and the first items added to the archives were scrapbooks. These books contain a variety of records, including programs and other printed ephemera, clipped reviews of plays produced, and important correspondence from the CPH Board of Trustees and professional staff to the membership and volunteers.

Scrapbooking was very popular in the nineteenth and early twentieth centuries. Two recent books on scrapbooking document this history quite thoroughly.[5] Just like any form of collecting, scrapbooking is a type of identity construction. The individual or group selecting the items to be pasted into a scrapbook is creating something that reflects the tastes and interests of the creator or creators. And more than other forms of record keeping, scrapbooks tell stories. Pasting records into the book format naturally lends itself to narrative construction and analysis, for those who "write" scrapbooks and for those who read them.

The selection and arrangement of the items pasted into the CPH scrapbooks offers a glimpse into the Play House culture that created them. For example, the second scrapbook, which documented the 1921–22 and 1922–23 seasons, gave extra space and attention to an unusual 1923 production of *Hamlet*, perhaps most notable because the "to be or not to be" monologue was omitted. The scrapbook documents more about this play than any other production that season, and includes bits of ephemera, such as a rather humorous hand-drawn cartoon about the gravedigger, and a costume design that compares the play to follies. This was a play that was typically seen as a vehicle for the great (and sometimes melodramatic) actors of the time, such as John Barrymore. Yet in the scrapbook selections, we see the CPH personnel reimagining the play as something more fun and less ponderous. All of this comes through in the choice of items placed in the scrapbook to document the production. These scrapbooks document the administrative history of the Play House as an institution, but as artifacts of the documentation strategy of the CPH volunteers, the scrapbooks also document the dynamic and creative processes of the Play House community.

Scrapbooks such as these were very common in the theater community at this time. Actors and actresses used them as documentation of their careers, clipping positive reviews that could later be used for self-promotional purposes.[6] Seen in a larger social context, scrapbooking was also important for a community that influenced the development of the Cleveland Play House; the women who were involved in founding the Play House were also suffragists. It is likely that their scrapbooking practice was informed by that movement.

Suffragists, as political outsiders, were deeply concerned with public image. Reviewing their publications and correspondence reveals that they encouraged one another to keep scrapbooks as a method of image management. By collecting periodical notices about her speeches and public appearances, a feminist activist could better understand the impact she was making on public support for women's suffrage. She could use the scrapbook to document changes over time. The battle for votes for women was long-fought, and maintaining documentation of incremental changes and positive press over the years helped suffragists keep their spirits up in the face of opposition.[7] Suffragists were also keenly aware of the historical value of scrapbooks and actively worked to ensure that their scrapbooks would be preserved in libraries and archives.

The women who founded the Play House and made its first scrapbooks would certainly have been familiar with suffragist scrapbooking practices. Just as the suffragists created scrapbooks not just for individual use, but to document the history of the movement, the CPH volunteers were documenting the history of a community in their scrapbooks.

Another element of the broader social culture surrounding the Play House was that it was founded by bohemians outside the cultural mainstream of conservative Cleveland society. These were modern artists performing for a small and exclusive audience. The founders of the Play House had every reason to believe that the Play House would eventually fail, and that its history would be lost if they did not take pains to preserve it. They believed that their work had artistic significance, and they wanted to ensure that it could be remembered. By reading the artifacts of this labor of documentation, we can see evidence of the different communities from which the Play House arose.

There is no doubt that these scrapbooks are worthy of preservation. The Cleveland Play House maintained its own records until 2011, when it donated its entire archives to Case Western Reserve University. The agreement guarantees that CWRU will continue to receive new records of permanent value as they become inactive at the Play House. Documenting the history of the CPH community, once an activity of a few female volunteers, is now a collaboration between the theater and the professional staff of the CWRU library. The Play House uses the records quite frequently in its publicity efforts. It is still deeply invested in telling its own story. But the records are also available to the people of Cleveland, to historians of theater, to individuals who want to learn as much as they can about their favorite actors or actresses, and to others who will use the records in ways we can't yet imagine.

The value of the CPH scrapbooks and the other records in the archives is substantially higher because the material retains its connection to the Cleveland Play House. The Play House community had been using its own records for almost one hundred years, and now new users are able to gain access to the collection through CWRU, and to learn about CPH through its institutional records and oral traditions. Researchers who travel to use the collection often also visit with Play House personnel during their trips to enrich their understanding of the records. While external use of the collection is fairly heavy, the materials still get the most use from the Play House staff. As an example, CPH is creating a series of YouTube videos that make use of information from the records and archival images to tell short stories about interesting moments in Play House history. These videos are distributed to CPH fans, who become secondary users of the archives as they watch. CPH fans, who support the Play House through ticket sales and donations, and drive the programming selections made by the Play House, are of course represented in the archival records as well. A fortunate consequence is that the lines between producers and consumers of archival material in the collection are blurring.

Our involvement with the CPH archives provides and promotes access to the collection to a much broader audience, including not only academic teachers and researchers, but also to users from the general community who may be interested in the material because of their own personal research interests. Thus the collection becomes a focal point for a community, all facilitated by the professional staff of the library who manage it. Our infrastructure to support scholarly research is well-suited to this kind of community building because we have the space, staff, and expertise to enable multiple kinds of access to the collection, and to enable the Play House to use its own materials more efficiently. For example, as the Play House prepared for its centennial year, we worked closely with it to develop programming to engage the local community around Play House history, growing the audience and support for the archives in a mutually beneficial way. Although as a research library we may have different goals and needs for the collection than the volunteers who created those first scrapbooks, we are able to support and build the community that they founded, validating their efforts to preserve their own history.

Integrating Collection-Based Collections into the Institutional Fabric

Many universities like CWRU emphasize research, teaching, and community service in their mission statements. Reflecting the parent institution's priorities, special collections in academic libraries have typically focused on supporting the internal research and teaching needs of the university. However, as relationships such as the one described here with the Cleveland Play House become more common, special collections will begin to align more closely with the institutional mission to serve its surrounding community.

Special collections can and should support communities by providing and promoting access to the history of those communities. This role can and should coexist with academic research and learning in our collections as well. Academic institutions historically have played a key role in the development of the communities in which they reside. Special collections can provide a context for community development, and the role the university played.

The role of the special collections librarian is to enable a meaningful, ongoing dialogue with collections at its core. The collection should become a platform for a new community of stakeholders: the producers of records, researchers, students, and other interested parties from the larger community who can become engaged in discourse with one another about the meaning and value of cultural artifacts. Such collections present a rich opportunity to position special collections librarians and archivists as leaders who connect our research institutions to local interests, and thereby describe and document our value.

Kate Theimer recently said in a talk about the participatory future of archives that "an organization focused on helping people, with great stories of their successes to share, has a better chance of surviving in today's economic environment."[8] Perhaps more important, community-based collections can enable us to create more meaningful relationships between people and cultural artifacts. To paraphrase my CWRU colleague Jill Tatem, we can use our collections and our expertise to build strong communities through awareness of shared history. This provides one of the most promising avenues for the future of special collection.

NOTES

1. Lee Anne George, "SPEC Survey Webcast on Community-Based Collections," Association of Research Libraries, July 8, 2015, www.arl.org/news/arl-news/3678.
2. William L. Joyce, "The Evolution of the Concept of Special Collections in American Research Libraries." *Rare Books and Manuscripts Librarianship* 3, no. 1 (1988): 19–29.
3. Steven Escar Smith, "From 'Treasure Room' to 'School Room': Special Collections and Education," *RBM: A Journal of Rare Books, Manuscripts, and Cultural Heritage* 7, no. 1 (2006): 31–39.
4. John H. Overholt, "Five Theses on the Future of Special Collections," *RBM: A Journal of Rare Books, Manuscripts, and Cultural Heritage* 14, no. 1 (2013): 15–20.
5. Ellen Gruber Garvey, *Writing with Scissors: American Scrapbooks from the Civil War to the Harlem Renaissance* (Oxford; New York: Oxford University Press, 2013); Susan Tucker, Katherine Ott, and Patricia Buckler, eds., *The Scrapbook in American Life* (Philadelphia: Temple University Press, 2006).
6. Garvey, 10.
7. Ibid., 172–206.
8. Kate Theimer, "The Future of Archives Is Participatory: Archives as Platform, or A New Mission for Archives," www.archivesnext.com/?p=3700.

CHAPTER 5

The Role of the Auction House

SELBY KIFFER

I work at Sotheby's as the International Senior Specialist for Books and Manuscripts, but I hold an MLS from Columbia University. I had intended to be an academic rare book librarian, but no library hired me.

The first meeting about the future of special collections that I attended was thirty years ago, which was held at the Grolier Club as part of its centennial celebration *Books and Prints, Past and Present*.[1] This was shortly after I graduated from Columbia, and it may be somewhat misleading to say that I attended the convocation. I was then working at the Grolier Club twenty hours a week as a general factotum, a position I called "Library Associate" on the resumes I was beginning to send out, and I was really there to see that the slide projectors were plugged in and that the speakers had pitchers of water handy.

A remark by Robert Giroux in his talk at that conference has always stayed me, and I think of it whenever I am at a similar conference, such as the 2001 Library of Congress symposium on special collections that I attended, not in an audiovisual role, but as a panelist. Giroux quoted Carl Van Doren's observation that "The future will never be futuristic. It will, of course, be like the present, only more so."[2]

In terms of special collections, I have found this to be true. The collectors are always getting older. Good material is always getting scarcer. Major dealers are retiring or dying, and they are not being replaced by dynamic young colleagues. Curricula and constituencies are always changing and need to be adapted. It can seem that the relationship between private collectors and institutional special collections really hasn't changed that much.

Yet I do see some real difference in private collecting since the 2001 conference at the Library of Congress. At the "Acknowledging the Past, Forging the Future" colloquium, Geoff Smith mentioned the two major options that private collectors have when it comes to the disposition of their books and manuscripts: sale (or, as Geoff more elegantly put it, redistribution) or donation. But increasingly collectors—the top tier, at least—are turning to a third option, which is perhaps a revival of an earlier course: establishing their own institutions or foundations.

I work with six major book and manuscript collectors, some quite closely, others much less frequently, each of whose collections I would value roughly at between $20,000,000 and $50,000,000. One of those collectors, I believe, is leaning towards donation; three are undecided; and two have pretty much decided that they are going to set up their own foundations. Part of the reason for these two collectors taking that step is that they have seen how materials are sometimes accepted by institutions on the basis of certain assurances and conditions granted to the donor, which later are not met. These collectors want to make sure that what they want to happen with their material is what happens. They want their collections to be preserved and maintained as a unit, but not in the context of an already established special collection within a university or library. That is one significant change that has occurred during the past three decades in the book world.

Of course, most collectors do not have collections that are worth between $20,000,000 and $50,000,000. Among other collectors I have noticed another change. In the past there were great collectors who collected in depth. However, there has been a growing general shift to what might be called "highlight collecting," in which collectors do not seek to form a comprehensive collection on a particular author or subject, but rather to focus on the accepted and codified masterworks.

When I started at Sotheby's, it seemed that offered in every book and manuscript sale were three items: the 1859 first edition of Darwin's *Origin of Species,* the 1814 Philadelphia official report of the Lewis and Clark expedition, and the first edition of *Moby-Dick* (but not its earlier three-decker London appearance as *The Whale*). In those sales, very good to fine copies could be purchased for $5,000 to $8,000—not a huge amount of money, even adjusted for the passage of time. Today, comparable copies of the *Origin* and the Lewis and Clark routinely sell for between $120,000 and $180,000. While *Moby-Dick* has not achieved that level, the increase in its value is still significant.

What has not occurred is a correlative rise in value for related publications concerning Lewis and Clark, for other of Herman Melville's novels, or for other of Charles Darwin's scientific monographs. One extreme, but by no means unique, example of this phenomenon starts with a sale at Sotheby's in 1977, when we offered Jonathan Goodwin's fantastic collection of modern literature. Ernest Hemingway was the author to which Goodwin was most devoted. Much like many collectors at that time, he wanted everything Hemingway wrote: juvenilia, periodical appearances, private publications, celebrated books, and critical failures. Two of his Hemingway titles, *The Sun Also Rises* and *The Torrents of Spring*, were inscribed by the author to Dr. Don Carlos Guffey, the obstetrician who had delivered the two children from Hemingway's marriage to Pauline Pfeiffer, Patrick and Gregory. In those innocent days, each book was estimated to sell for between $700 and $900; or perhaps even then auction estimates tended to be modest.

In the Goodwin sale, *The Sun Also Rises* sold for $6,000, and *The Torrents of Spring* sold for $4,500—a bit less, certainly, but still in the same level of magnitude. Both books were purchased by the same collector, Maurice Neville, who, in turn, consigned his library to Sotheby's in 2004. By this time, the shift in collecting from comprehensive to highlights could already be recognized. In fairness, there is often a reason for selectivity in collecting. I (and I suspect most persons at this symposium) have read *The Sun Also Rises*. I, and I suspect most others, have not read *The Torrents of Spring*. Those who have read it indicate that it is largely a parody of Sherwood Anderson and was likely written to allow Hemingway to get out of a contract with Boni & Liveright—Anderson's publisher—and sign with Charles Scribner.

In 2004, we estimated the value of *The Sun Also Rises* at $80,000 to $120,000 and *The Torrents of Spring* at $40,000 to $60,000. *The Sun Also Rises* sold for $370,000 and *The Torrents of Spring* passed, without a single bid, at $28,000. That is stark evidence of a very real change in collecting practices within less than two decades. As more and more dollars chase fewer and fewer available copies of the same books, private collections could become less and less relevant to building special collections.

In Jay Satterfield's contribution to this book (see chapter 14), he notes that the Dartmouth College library special collections are not there just to show cool stuff. However, the fact is cool stuff is exactly what attracts private collectors, and it is what presents opportunities for special collections. Certainly to the extent that special collections will continue to be guided by private collectors, the already established movement away from traditional books and manuscripts and towards the material of popular culture will only intensify. Yet, often these materials are not only the ones that appeal to private collectors, but that also can attract readers and visitors to special collections.

The most expensive manuscript that Sotheby's sold in 2014 was not by Abraham Lincoln, George Washington, Thomas Jefferson, or Benjamin Franklin. It was the autograph lyrics to "Like A Rolling Stone" by Bob Dylan, which sold for just under $2,000,000. Three years ago, on the same day that we sold Robert Kennedy's copy of the Emancipation Proclamation signed by Lincoln for a little bit less than $4,000,000, we also sold James Naismith's two-page typescript of the founding rules of basketball for a little bit more than $4,000,000. This is further evidence that there has been a shift in what private collectors consider important, or at least in what they consider cool.

Recently listed on abebooks.com was a copy of the *Beauties of Swift: or, the Favorite Offspring of Wit & Genius*, published in London in 1782. The book has a preface, not by, but addressed to Samuel Johnson, which could generate a bit of added interest for a Johnson completest. This copy is bound in contemporary calf, and a bit tired. The price, when converted from pounds to dollars, was $83.23. In 2010, Sotheby's sold a copy in somewhat better condition for more than a thousand times that: $102,000. Why? The copy Sotheby's sold was from the library at Mount Vernon, it had George Washington's bookplate, and it had George Washington's signature on the title-page.

What that book and that copy did not have was any great research value. Books from Washington's library turn up with some frequency, although this particular volume had not been sold publicly since 1891.

Sotheby's resold that book in 2013 for the private collector who purchased it in 2010. Over the past thirty years he had bought seven books, including the *Swift*, which had been in Washington's library and were signed by him. The seller had paid between $18,000 and $102,000 for each of these books. Sotheby's offered the seven titles as a package and were able to say that they represented the largest group of books from George Washington's library to be offered in a single sale since 1904. They sold for $1,200,000—and they were purchased by a special collections library: The Fred W. Smith National Library for the Study of George Washington at Mount Vernon.

I would like to think that Mount Vernon's purchase supports my notion that it can be appropriate for libraries to spend money on books that produce a sense of wonder and that don't necessarily address the curriculum. Books like this also help me fight off the doubts that sometimes beset me that books and manuscripts are intrinsically boring. I don't really believe that, of course, but I can say that I have been to a lot of boring book and manuscript exhibitions, and I would bet that some readers of this book have as well.

During the Case Western Reserve University colloquium at which my presentation was originally given, I was struck by the extent to which librarians, booksellers, members of book departments at auction houses, and everyone else involved with antiquarian books has something in common that I had not previously recognized: we are all competing with *paintings*, whether that means museums, art galleries, or, in my case, colleagues in contemporary, modern, and impressionist departments who more than once have sold a single work of art for more than $100,000,000. A former colleague of mine, Tobias Meyer, who was the head of contemporary art at Sotheby's, once said in an interview, "My job is to make art expensive." I have never felt that way about books, but I do think that we all have an obligation to make books and manuscripts more exciting.

During the colloquium, Malcolm E. O'Hagan, President of the American Writers Museum, said that unless they are given some context, visitors to the Library of Congress spend about ten seconds looking at the Gutenberg Bible. Initially that sounds very discouraging. However, the more I thought about it, I wondered if that is really so different from the museum experience of many visitors? We've all seen people breeze through a gallery without really taking in what they are looking at. And yet people, including tourists and families, feel that they ought to go to museums. We need to inculcate that same attitude towards special collection libraries.

Like it or not, it has to be acknowledged that monetary value plays a role in all of this. In November 2013, Sotheby's sold one of the eleven surviving copies of the Bay Psalm Book, the first book printed in British America and the first book printed in English in the New World. Prior to the auction, Sotheby's took the book on an exhibition tour, during which it was shown at the Rosenbach Museum and Library in Philadelphia, the Cleveland Public Library, the Newberry Library in Chicago, the Dallas Public Library, the St. Louis Mercantile, and the Doheny Memorial Library at the University of Southern California. During these exhibitions it was gratifying to see the number of people who came to see the book, many of whom travelled a significant distance, and to see the visceral recognition they exhibited that somehow this unassuming little book was very important. At most stops there were entire families lining up to try to read whatever passage I had opened the book to (most frequently Psalm 23). In St. Louis and Los Angeles there were many students taking selfies with the psalter.

Undoubtedly, one reason so many people came to see the Bay Psalm Book was the chance to see a book that was estimated to be going for sale for $15,000,000. In the event it actually sold for $14,200,000, purchased by someone who insists he is not a collector, David Rubenstein, who has said that he eventually plans to give the book to an institution. Several years ago, David Rubenstein bought a 1297 manuscript of the Magna Carta, which had been on deposit and exhibition at the National Archives, which he has put back on deposit and exhibition at the National Archives. Perhaps the future does not lie with collectors who specifically are building special collections, but more generally with philanthropists.

Finally, value—or the potential for value—also plays a role in uncovering lost or forgotten treasures. People do not call Sotheby's to find out the format of their book or to find out whether its binding is contemporary with the date of its publication. What they want to know is what it is worth. Most of the time the subject of the call or email isn't worth anything, but sometimes it is. Sometimes that curiosity about the value of an object can lead to unexpected results, such as when Sotheby's was asked to identify four autograph notebooks by Walt Whitman that had been missing since World War II from the Library of Congress (and to which they were repatriated). Or discovering that the first half of the autograph manuscript of *Adventures of Huckleberry Finn,* which had been believed to have been destroyed—because Mark Twain said that it had been destroyed—was actually safe in the attic of a house in the suburbs of Los Angeles. Today that portion of the manuscript has been reunited with the second half of the holograph in the Buffalo Public Library.

In the final analysis, any event, any sale, any discovery, any publicity that focuses the attention of the public on books and manuscripts—on the significance, value, or capacity of those books to evoke awe—is good for private collectors and special collections alike, and helps to ensure a positive future for library special collections.

NOTES

1. The proceedings of that conference were published as *Grolier Club. Books and Prints, Past and Future: Papers Presented at the Grolier Club Centennial Convocation 26–28 April 1984* (New York: Grolier Club, 1984).
2. Robert Giroux, "The Future of the Book," in *Grolier Club. Books and Prints, Past and Future,* 54. In this essay, Giroux notes that the original remark by Van Doren was relayed in private conversation.

CHAPTER 6

Forging into the Future

Facing Digital Realities and Forecasting Endeavors for Special Collections Librarianship

ATHENA N. JACKSON

This essay expands upon and captures the spirit of a talk I presented at the panel "Special Collections in the Age of Digital Scholarship" at the "Acknowledging the Past, Forging the Future" colloquium held at Case Western Reserve University in the fall of 2014. My talking points focused on my trajectory into the field and the overarching shifts in digitization efforts I have encountered. As our profession has grown, so has our understanding of our roles and the potential for partnering with students and scholars in digital projects. In this corollary essay, I will briefly review the trends (insofar as they can be considered trends at this point; perhaps they are better described as forecasts), I foresee with respect to representing our collections to a digitally focused audience, as well as in participating in deep scholarship via digital technologies.

The panel was asked to respond to the lecture presented by Stephen Enniss, Director of the Harry Ransom Center (see chapter 13), who aimed to explore the future of the book as object: how it will look, how it will be collected, and what needs to be collected and preserved today to ensure its longevity. He also examined the emerging role and value of special collections in a world of digital scholarship, and how digital scholarship techniques can complement and advance the use of manuscripts, rare books, and other archival materials in all formats, including images, art work, and audio and video files. I have further considered this prompt over the past several months in light of our panel discussion at the colloquium. The essay below encompasses portions of my talk, combined with broader observations about the progress of digitization efforts.

Let us first consider the changes in our collections and profession. Rare books and manuscripts are certainly valued assets in special collections that should be documented and preserved for research. But now there is a growing emphasis on developing collections that represent various cultures, impressions, and interests beyond the typical canonical endeavors historically set forth in US academic libraries. We also have embraced a focus on temporality and provenance that includes cultural sensitivity and historical agency for heretofore silenced or unrepresented voices. We now fill historical gaps and surface the ideas of lesser-known perspectives of and grassroots reactions to the humanistic record. Our existing collections of works and papers of men and women of letters now include new neighbors whose provenance stems from the common voices of contemporary eras and, often, of community or cultural groups whose ideas and legacies were yet to be incorporated into the historical record until brought into the archive. Moreover, we aspire to recruit colleagues from underrepresented communities to ensure that perspectives and initiatives span the scope of our changing demographics. We have been proactive in these roles in the last decade and the results of our endeavors have visibly changed our professional composition and the multifaceted cultural heritage histories we document. Taking this into consideration, prioritizing digitization projects and promoting digital scholarship must acknowledge the wide range of collections we steward for research communities of digitally savvy and multicultural patrons.

I have been involved in a range of planned digitization projects from the small-scale boutique and project-driven to the large-scale digitization efforts of a Big Ten school where several units work together on different types of digitization projects across many platforms. All of this is buttressed by my experience on the corporate side of these types of projects in terms of how I approach the planning, piloting, and execution of digitization projects using unpublished, sometimes difficult to describe, and always historically relevant materials. In my current position, I find ways to streamline, codify, and create transparency for those processes that enhance the descriptive, interpretive, and magical moments that occur during research that takes place in the reading room and the classroom, which are often translated to the digital realm. Underscoring all of my work and professional drive is my background as member of an underrepresented community. As a Latina, a special collections librarian, an active member in our professional community, and an administrator who is committed to understanding the hybridized nature of the analog and digital work we do every day, I humbly submit that I represent a glimpse into the future of our profession. It is from this perspective that I will share the trajectory of my career as a case study for present and future digital scholarship trends in the field.

I came to the analog from the digital from an unusual background that has shaped my approach to my work as a special collections professional. In the early twenty-first century, I began my career as an indexer for an electronic publisher of digital humanities collections designed to meet unique academic research needs in an online environment. Little did I know at the time that I was participating in the earliest phases of what would now be described as digital scholarship or digital humanities, employing humanistic approaches to data mining and refined indexing. I learned a corporate model of creating what is now a common product in the library world: the digital collection, which we now often create ourselves for our research communities. I managed talented indexers who performed close readings of historical resources to provide refined and relevant topical access that established the expectations researchers now have when using databases and online catalogs. When I worked in electronic publishing in the early days of what could be considered digital humanities scholarship, the programmers, indexers, editors, and editorial advisors had direct access to one another so that their products included dynamic approaches to developing databases.

I felt such a passion for my work that I left to get a library degree with a plan to return and continue the same career path in e-publishing. However, it was during a special collections course in library school that I realized my personal vocation was for the academic library. After discovering my professional ethos to be more aligned with academic librarianship, I began my library career working on digital projects in a state archive and then moved into an NEH-funded newspaper digitization project in collaboration with the Library of Congress at Louisiana State University.

After this initial foray into the field through soft-money projects, I segued into a more typical special collections librarian position, where I was responsible for curating and teaching with rare books, and often participated in digitization of archival materials. I curated exhibitions, developed a unit blog, and performed reader services for students, faculty, and researchers. As my expertise grew, I moved into a more administrative role in my current position as Associate Director of the Special Collections Library at the University of Michigan.

At Michigan, I have spent the last year working on the Special Collections Image Bank, where we provide access to public domain images scanned in response to incidental requests by patrons and staff. This year, I am piloting a digital scholarship program derived from an unpublished think piece I wrote to crystallize my small team's goals, centered on thinking beyond capturing "*Figure 1.*" The goal for this project is to move beyond supporting a patron in her search for an image (i.e., to acquire the image for "*see Figure 1*" in narratives), which we will of course continue to support. However, we want to extend our service further to support digital analysis of those images that did not make it into the patron's research but still supported her arguments. As our researchers have been snapping digital images for their own post-visit analyses in the reading room, I have been wondering what we can do to partner with them more proactively. What more can they explore beyond just the one image selected (the common, "see *Figure 1*") to make a strong argument in a publication or assignment? How can we harness our efforts toward answering a question like that in order to make our services visible to our audiences and relevant to our stakeholders? I hope the discussions borne from the colloquium and those inspired by this publication will provide some ideas about our future. I honestly do not think it will be bleak or passionless, but offers the potential for making sense of some of our pioneering moments and professionally tectonic experiences while still holding on to the "exuberant chaos" of our work, as another colloquium speaker, Jay Satterfield, so aptly put it (see chapter 14).

What skills will special collections librarians need to expose confidently and responsibly the historical record and our collective cultural heritage online to constituencies who are increasingly comfortable accessing digital surrogates of primary source materials? Moreover, what techniques should we deploy to cultivate digital scholarship that begins in the reading room or classroom, where we act as partners by extending our service throughout the research process?

Should we learn all the technical skills needed to do this? I say, not necessarily. Do we make bold outreaches to our colleagues in the library, who know key techniques that could surface a different approach to reader services and instruction that includes options for data mining surrogate images from our rare and archival collections? I say, yes.

I know I am not alone in asking these questions, and I suggest that our unique collections and our existing resources dictate our actions as we move forward in this activity in our respective institutions. There is no one set pace or single lane for this work. As I said at the colloquium, I have more questions than answers. And, I hope by opening a dialogue that begins with many questions we can find common ground in our work, and build partnerships with one another.

Academic libraries have embraced technical expertise and skills that have influenced a wave of new approaches to expanding our reach into the electronic ether. Special collections libraries and their curators, archivists, outreach and education librarians, public services staff, and catalogers have had to accommodate this shift in their approaches to describing their materials outside of the reading room by designing instruction spaces and creating finding aids, catalogs, and physical exhibitions, to name a few. I purposefully think broadly about the term "skills" rather than focusing on "technical skills." Indeed, we can and have nurtured the latter in our special collections colleagues, and much has and still can be written as digitization approaches continue to shift around procedures, digital curation and preservation, and interoperability. Best practices, workshops, and social media flourish with opportunities to expose and grow one's skillset in our field. Even to someone of my generation who observed humanistic digital research endeavors in earlier states, the technical aspects of our field can be daunting. Learning these skills is becoming a noble vocation in itself.

It is worth noting that, given the ways we have already captured and codified data to describe materials typically found in a closed stack setting, it is of utmost importance not to discount or remove these efforts when exposing digital surrogates from our collections in contemporary scholarship. Bibliographic knowledge and fundamental archival skills still matter. Our profession is rooted in an ethos of which we should all be proud: we strive not to be the arbiters of history, but the advocates for the historical record. It is this foundation upon which I build all of my efforts and continue to exercise the practices of descriptive bibliography, taxonomical analysis, and archival assessment while at the same time exploring activities with my metadata and digital scholarship colleagues to find where our skills and missions intersect.

Thus, my perspective is one that constantly considers how we devise ways to engender digital access, and more crucially, how we endeavor to shrink the digital divide (of both access and application) while disabusing our constituencies of the thankfully already fading notion that our collections are reserved only for an elite class and only in the reading room. Happily, proactive outreach of all types will, and already is, starting to shape perceptions of our efforts, our relevance, and our collective missions. In fact, I posit that with digital social outreach (as demonstrated by our pioneering colleagues already engaged in these activities), we have an opportunity to enable access for communities who would be reticent to visit our reading rooms without such intentionality on our parts.[1] Our community outreach activities via social media promote the collection highlights, the remarkably relevant, and the quotidian (to us) work behind our endeavors. Couple these with building partnerships with our students, faculty, scholars, and enthusiasts through pointed and extended service, and we potentially have a paradigm of new approaches to the work taking place in our settings.

Put simply, answering the questions that surfaced in the colloquium segment "Special Collections in an Age of Digital Scholarship" will require a sense of moving beyond just providing access and serving digital copies of analog resources (or born-digital access in these more common times). We must continue to deploy and advocate for our skills with emphasis on providing context and primary source research expertise when partnering with digital scholars of the humanistic record. Indeed, it is time to shake a perceived (and very wrong) notion that when one thinks of special collections the adjoining epithets of "elite" or "forbidden" to describe our holdings and/or services can be far removed from the modern researcher's awareness. It will take a certain amount of flexibility to adjust nimbly to digital humanities, whose products are experimental approaches to analyzing data. Engagement will be less orchestrated and sometimes even messy. However, the potential benefits are already apparent. There will be more opportunities to cultivate new scholarship, new champions for the historical record, and new collections where all voices—whose context and relevance are captured with our expertise—are heard at the reading room table and in the electronic ether.

NOTE

1. The University of Iowa's Special Collections tumblr (http://uispeccoll.tumblr.com/) is a fantastic example of how many colleagues have made strides in bringing collections into the social media present. The Folger Shakespeare Library also showcases the many ways to stay connected; see www.folger.edu/connect-with-the-folger.

The Enduring Object

Digital scholarship methods are changing how we collect physical materials, and how users interact with them.

CHAPTER 7

Lawrence Clark Powell Revisited

The Functions of Rare Books Today

JOEL SILVER

> *Rare books have a function; they can be made to serve no less than the battered texts in the reserve book room. A librarian who would minimize rare books to the point of exclusion in the so-called functional library, is merely revealing his own unfamiliarity with certain practical functions which can be served by rare books.*[1]

Lawrence Clark Powell's impassioned defense of rare books in library collections appeared just over seventy-five years ago in the inaugural issue of *College and Research Libraries*. Surely, no such polemic for the importance of rare books would be needed now, after more than three-quarters of a century of efforts by devoted special collections librarians across the country to build small and large special collections departments, and to integrate rare books into teaching and research at all levels.

Our world today is a long way from the one that Powell knew in 1939. Most things in libraries have changed greatly since he wrote, and the typical academic library of 2015 is unrecognizably different from the ones that Powell knew in the 1940s and 1950s, when he served as UCLA's University Librarian, and as Director of the William Andrews Clark Memorial Library. What Powell regarded as the essence of any research library—the book collection—is seen increasingly by some librarians as an expensive and space-wasting anachronism, consulted chiefly by a rapidly aging group of emeriti and other Luddite-leaning users. Most of the "battered texts in the reserve book room" were replaced long ago by remotely accessible digital versions, and today's academic librarians are busy trying to figure out what the "functional library" of today actually is and does, and what it is that they're supposed to be doing now to serve their users.

Special collections have never been more active or more visible. Library deans and directors, though some of them no longer have the word "library" in their job titles, have realized that special collections hold interesting and photogenic objects, and that they also have great potential for attracting donors and serving as venues for events. Powell certainly recognized this in 1939, and many of the activities promoted and discussed at the 2014 colloquium "Acknowledging the Past, Forging the Future," from outreach to students, faculty, and the general public, and collecting locally and with an eye to the future, were advocated by Powell in his article.

But some things haven't changed in the intervening years, including the tension between special collections departments and other departments within research libraries, and the ongoing competition for dwindling resources shows no signs of abating. Many of the acquisitions and publications endowments within library systems are earmarked for special collections materials, and it's easy for underfunded colleagues to become jealous of the high-profile purchases and the often more luxurious surroundings that many special collections enjoy. Another thing that hasn't changed is the desire of librarians to measure their success by statistics, whether this involves books circulated, readers served, or web pages viewed. By practically any statistical measure, special collections departments will always come up woefully short, but these statistics can't measure the intangible impact that rare books and manuscripts can have on people who are directly exposed to their magic.

Though rare books and manuscripts have no shortage of competitors these days for the attention of students or the general public, they do turn up in surprising places, most notably on some of the reality television shows that feature antiques, including *Antiques Roadshow, American Pickers,* and *Pawn Stars.* All of these shows owe their success to a combination of entertainment and information, with the regulars and visiting experts discussing the attributes and collecting appeal of a remarkable variety of items, along with the constant hook of well-paced details about popularity, market value, and salability.

As I write, the television network History (formerly The History Channel) is preparing to premiere an episode of *Pawn Stars* entitled "Personal Collection," in which the featured family members discuss some of their own favorite pieces. As the program's website states:

> Get personal with the Pawn Stars and discover the items they've most wanted for themselves: a motorcycle once owned by Rick's idol, Steve McQueen, a diamond encrusted 2004 Super Bowl Ring from the New England Patriots, a rare 1484 incunable book, and a 1986 Buick that leaves Chum "regally" impressed.[2]

Special collections libraries, many of which hold "incunable books" such as the Thomas Aquinas *Summa Theologiae* featured on the show, couldn't buy this kind of promotional publicity. When rare books can hold their own on television in the company of Steve McQueen's motorcycle or a Patriots' Super Bowl ring, they've reached a level both of coolness and public awareness that Lawrence Clark Powell could only dream of. Powell knew, though, that it was up to librarians themselves not only to preserve what they had, and to bring these riches to the notice and attention of others, but to think creatively and not limit themselves to a preconceived role:

> Milton observed that books are not dead things. My observation is that often their custodians are. Because of their historical significance, their intrinsic value, their beauty, and sentimental associations, rare books, when intelligently grouped, have power to excite the imagination and stimulate the intellectual curiosity of the student. A rare book collection, no matter how modest, can be made by alert librarians to play an educational role, and to enliven the library, increase its prestige, and to draw alumni and friends....
>
> Funds are not the important thing in collecting a contemporary's works and memorabilia; what is necessary is vision, courage, discrimination, and enthusiasm. It pains me to think of Emily Dickinson and Herman Melville having had to wait until the next century after them for any widespread recognition. "Surely," one says, "you do not hold our librarian predecessors responsible for that! Literary discovery and

popularization are the proper function of critics, not librarians." "Very well, then," I reply, "you would have librarians remain mere custodians, technicians and administrators. It is true that that is what we have largely been in the past. Now there must be a new vision, or we will perish. And there is a new vision taking form out of the searching scrutinies to which we are subjecting our profession. This gives me confidence in our future."[3]

What Powell wrote seems somewhat less radical today than it must have in 1939, but if things are better now, it's because Powell and others of his generation helped to make it so. Powell, who died at the age of 94 in 2001, never stopped writing about the magic of books, and he never stopped reminding librarians that theirs is a service profession, which has the power, like the books we acquire, preserve, and make available, to transform people's lives. This work is far from complete, and in a world in which libraries and books are no longer considered inseparable companions, it's more important than ever that librarians take advantage of the power that their ever-expanding collections hold.

A famous story, which was often repeated in library circles in various versions during Powell's day, deserves to be better known today. During the planning and construction of Yale University's Sterling Memorial Library, University Librarian Andrew Keogh is said to have suggested that an inscription to be carved above the new library's entrance should read: "This is not the Yale Library. *That* is inside." And for special collections librarians, no matter what else we might do in the digital realm, the essence of Keogh's statement is still true. It's the collections, not the pictures of the collections, that comprise the library, and we're in the privileged position of being able to share them with more people than ever. As long as we continue to realize this, I, like Lawrence Clark Powell, also have confidence in our future.

NOTES

1. Lawrence Clark Powell, "The Functions of Rare Books," College and Research Libraries 1, no. 1 (December 1939), 97.
2. *Pawn Stars*, "Personal Collection," www.history.com/shows/pawn-stars/season-11/episode-40?watch=true.
3. Powell, 101–03.

CHAPTER 8

Special Collections Libraries and the Uses of the Past

(Apologies to Herbert Muller)

PAUL RUXIN

That famous Santayana warning about the past tells only half the story; sometimes repeating the past offers not doom, but promise. Although the lessons of the past are as useful a tool for special collections libraries and librarians as they are for other institutions and people, the collections themselves are the past, not merely remnants or memories, but survivors. What follows are merely three examples of how the special collections libraries of the future can benefit, and benefit their future clients, from paying attention to what has gone before.

On April 4, 2001, two divisions of the Library of Congress, the Center for the Book, and Rare Book and Special Collections, sponsored a Rare Book Forum at the Library. Moderated by Mark Dimunation, it presented three speakers, Alice Schreyer of the University of Chicago, special collections and rare book librarian; Bill Reese, of William Reese Company, dealer; and Robert Jackson, of Cleveland, collector and philanthropist. Their presentations are available and very much worth seeking out.[1] All three papers are thoughtful and carry messages perhaps even more important now than when originally delivered.

Among the several points they addressed that current special collections libraries must confront today, one stands out: special collections libraries were seldom "collected" through patient acquisitions over many years by the libraries and their librarians. Building a collection requires a dedicated collector, a budget, and time. Great collections have most often been assembled by great collectors—Folger, Morgan, Huntington, Hyde-Eccles—and have by gift become part of institutional special collection libraries, which have continued to enhance the original gift. Some libraries, like the Newberry, are rightfully proud of being a "collection of collections," representing many significant gifts, and purchases of collections built by others (e.g., the Harmsworth collection at Folger, or the Silver collection at Newberry. In general though, great collections have been built by collectors, not by librarians).

While there are still great private collections and collectors, the golden age of collecting is in the past. Moreover, many collectors, now as always, are torn between two altruistic impulses—the first, to preserve their collection intact for the use of future scholars, the second, to have their collection dispersed for the pleasure of future collectors. While both paths offer opportunities for special collection libraries, it is also true, as Bill Reese pointed out in 2001, that over time the supply of "rare" books—the heart of what makes a collection special—is shrinking, as they disappear into institutions, never again to be available for acquisition. Fewer collectors, fewer collections, fewer books—surely these are among the challenges libraries must meet in attending to the "we must build it so they will come" part of their mission. These circumstances make building relationships with collectors more important than ever, as acquisition budgets and potential donors both reflect diminishing numbers. The three speakers at the Library of Congress in 2001, had much good advice on this subject (as does Jon Lindseth, whose remarks are included in chapter 3 of this volume).

Let me offer some suggestions for meeting these challenges. First, special collections are not and ought not become museums. The books and manuscripts they contain are there to be used, not to be worshipped as relics. "Building" special collections must thus be broadly understood. In this context "building" is not limited to acquiring, displaying, and preserving the books and manuscripts themselves, but must also include encouraging collectors as well as cultivating, building bridges, and opening conversations among the libraries, and the collectors, dealers, and scholars whose collaboration will produce special collections that can achieve their optimal use when ultimately housed in a special collection library.

Chapter 8: Special Collections Libraries and the Uses of the Past

Special collections librarians must regard establishing personal relationships with collectors, as well as with dealers, as a significant responsibility within their job descriptions. Major gifts, after all, seldom come from strangers. "Building" collections must also include expanding access to an expanded audience of potential users. Cataloging previously unfindable material and digitizing previously untouchable, fragile paper or parchment are the equivalents of acquiring something new. If the point of special collections is to preserve their holdings for use, rather than simply for viewing in exhibition cases, libraries, collectors, dealers, scholars, conservators, and technology experts must see themselves as part of the same enterprise, and must come to know each other, to respect each other, to encourage each other, and to work together.

In August 2014 Florida Polytechnic University (FPU) opened a library in a building designed by Santiago Calatrava. It contains a "digital" library (reportedly of 135,000 volumes), but it houses no physical books. The Director of Libraries at FPU called it "a boldly relevant decision to go forward without books."[2] Relevant to what, the press release did not say. Surprisingly a "policy analyst" for the American Library Association said that "Digital is in some ways better. People can find things easier [sic],[3] and more important, observing with dismay that, 'in the past, you could buy a...book and it could sit on your shelf for 120 years." Yes it could. And it could be filled with unexpected treasures of history, or evidences of ownership or usage, until discovered by a reader or user never imagined by the acquiring librarian over a century earlier. That future discoverer, however unexpected or tardy, will be engaged, delighted, and informed by the unexpected gift of finding it, holding it, and examining it closely for the evidence that proves that books—physical books, the essence of special collections—are timeless. The lesson of FPU and its admirers is for us to understand how wrong they are, how important it is that a book may be "found" even if, or perhaps only if, after 120 years. That possibility is, of course, a *raison d'etre* of special collections libraries.

On February 25, 1987, David Vander Meulen gave the Engelhard lecture at the Library of Congress, entitled *Where Angels Fear to Tread: Descriptive Bibliography and Alexander Pope*. The special collections library will continue to be important long into the future, for many reasons, but Vander Meulen helps us understand several of these. First, despite their digitization, original materials will continue to be indispensable primary source material. As anyone who has used EEBO, ECCO, Hathi Trust, or Google Books images will know, digitization is far from perfect—whole pages are often missing, or illegible. Second, many of these digital databases are prohibitively expensive. Special collections libraries and their parent institutions, and smaller colleges and universities often lack the money necessary to purchase the costly access by subscription necessary to make them available to their own users. Thus, physical books will remain important for a long time, until questions of both access and accuracy have been addressed.

Equally important is the fact of the object itself. There is certainly an emotional and subjective response to the intellectual experience of reading it, which is enhanced by holding a 1623 First Folio, as compared to viewing it on a screen. But this aspect of the importance of the object is less pressing, less universal, and, frankly, less easy to justify in any objective way than another aspect of the physical book that Vander Meulen helps us appreciate. In this aspect of its mission, the special collection library of the future has an important and perhaps unique role to play in the world of scholarship and learning. It can be—it ought to be—the center for the underutilized, underappreciated, understudied, but profoundly learned, discipline of descriptive bibliography. Descriptive bibliography has been around for a relatively short time in the history of the book, even if we go back to the seminal work of Fredson Bowers and, later, Philip Gaskell and Thomas Tanselle. I believe that at one time, PhD degree candidates in English were expected to have a working knowledge of it. Such masters as Frederick Pottle and Richard Fleeman in the mid-twentieth century created magisterial works of bibliography, without which much of the subsequent research and scholarship in their chosen subjects could not have been accomplished. It is not possible, in my opinion, to be a serious collector, dealer, or special collections librarian without some mastery of the language, semiotics, and notation of formal, descriptive bibliography. This is because the physical object itself carries information that must essentially be decoded and understood to extract from the book its full intellectual value.

Vander Meulen's talk at the Library of Congress was about his then ongoing (perhaps it still is, in the sense that a bibliographer's work is never done) bibliography of Pope's *The Dunciad*. His is a truly magnificent achievement, but at the time of his talk it was very much a work in progress. At the time he had reviewed 800 copies of 33 editions of *The Dunciad*. Why is that important? What was the process he followed? Why does it matter for the future relationship between special collection libraries and descriptive bibliography? Here is part of his description of what he did to distinguish among the copies. He used a micrometer to

> measure paper thickness—first the total bulk of all the leaves that had passed through a press. Then I also measured the thickness of each leaf at the center of each of its three outside edges. As a result, I hoped to offer quantitative data for what Griffith [an earlier bibliographer] had pointed to only in relative terms: he had distinguished issues of Pope's *Works* in 1717, for instance, as being on a "second royal" paper, on "still thicker" royal paper, and on "a very thick" royal paper.[4]

What Vander Meulen learned from this is as important as what he did not; in fact,

> the average thickness of a large number of samples of the same paper differed from the average thickness of another variety, [but] the variation within the same paper...was too great for the result to serve as a trustworthy means of discriminating varieties.[5]

But he also measured the exact size of each leaf, which enabled him to check his tally of chain lines, which in turn enabled him "to make discoveries about these books that simply would have been impossible otherwise."

While "smell-o-vision" may someday be an enhanced feature of digitization, we are a long way from the time when digitization will allow collectors and scholars to feel, touch, and measure with precision the objects we care so much about. Until then descriptive bibliography will be in large part dependent on having the books themselves, and scholars and librarians and collectors will be dependent on the collections that can be described only by such bibliographic efforts. Special collection libraries ought to shape their own futures by reemphasizing descriptive bibliography; reintroducing their librarians and users to the concepts and principles of descriptive bibliography; teaching how the book as information and the book as thing, the book as text and the book as object, are integrated by descriptive bibliography, thus enhancing their value for all who collect and learn from them. Special collections libraries must become not only repositories, but also teaching centers. Instruction in descriptive bibliography ought to be widely available in the very places it can best be applied and used. As a collector, my own rudimentary knowledge of descriptive bibliography has served me well. It has allowed me to identify books to a certainty well beyond what truncated and often erroneous catalog or dealer descriptions suggested, and to buy, or not buy, accordingly. Think what a real grasp of its principles could do for the librarian and scholar.

The answer to why descriptive bibliography is important to the broader community engaged with special collections is, once again, best described by Vander Meulen. Using the tools provided by descriptive bibliography results in

> involvement [that] leads to the most fulfilling pleasure of all, the excitement of engaging in the historical reconstruction of these works. It is an activity that requires those much-discussed eighteenth-century qualities of reason and imagination. It is a process that brings us not only closer to the minds and actions of those who manufactured the books but also, ultimately into the presence of Alexander Pope himself.[6]

NOTES

1. The three talks were published as *Collectors & Special Collections—Three Talks* (Washington, DC: Library of Congress, 2002). Alice Schreyer's talk was also published separately as *Elective Affinities: Private Collectors & Special Collections in Libraries* (Chicago: University of Chicago Library, 2001).
2. Letitia Stein, "Library without Books Debuts at Florida's Newest College," August 25, 2014, www.reuters.com/article/2014/08/25/us-usa-florida-library-idUSKBN0GP0W620140825.
3. Ibid.
4. David L. Vander Meulen, *Where Angels Fear to Tread: Descriptive Bibliography and Alexander Pope* (Washington, DC: Library of Congress, 1988), 16.
5. Ibid., 17.
6. Ibid., 28.

CHAPTER 9

Everything Old Is New Again

Transformation in Special Collections

ALICE SCHREYER

> *Don't throw the past away*
> *You might need it some rainy day*
> *Dreams can come true again*
> *When everything old is new again.*[1]

Works that achieve the status of "classics" sustain—perhaps demand—rereading. This is the enduring value of rare books: just as readers across time and place discover something new, strange, and illuminating in the text of a classic, physical books present endless opportunities for new ways of looking and learning. As the final line of the verse by Peter Allen and Carol Bayer Sager suggests, in special collections, "everything old is new again."

The last two decades in special collections have been "transformative," the term used by Judge Barrington Parker in a June 10, 2014, decision for the US Court of Appeals for the Second Circuit.[2] He upheld the decision by Judge Harold Baer, for the US District Court for the Southern District of New York, that creation of a searchable, full-text database counts as fair use and does not infringe copyright, as the Author's Guild had claimed. The ruling determined that "a use could be transformative if the function or purpose of the use is different from that of the original work."[3] In making a corpus of digitized texts available for use by persons with print disabilities and for keyword searching, the HathiTrust transforms books into something very different from what was intended by their creators, and thus does not violate the copyrights of authors.

The transformation of special collections, however, has been quite intentional. We have "authored" our own work, embracing energetic outreach and interactive teaching to bring students—especially undergraduates—into newly designed, technology-equipped classrooms. Support from granting agencies–especially the Council on Library and Information Resources (CLIR), with funding from the Andrew W. Mellon Foundation—enabled many libraries to reduce arrearages substantially, encouraging adoption of new approaches to archival processing and book cataloging that provide for different levels of description depending on the type of material and how likely it is to be used. And we consider pedagogical value to be an important criterion in collection development, recognizing that our collections must support diverse subjects of current teaching interest, even in areas where we do strive to build a comprehensive research collection.

As we continue to uncover hidden collections (and our work is far from complete), we are also seeking ways to expand digital access. Our initial concern that digital surrogates might diminish interest in originals has long since faded. We now realize that they attract and satisfy the needs of new audiences at the same time as they fulfill different study, research, and teaching needs for those who also consult originals. Digitization is fast becoming an expectation, not an add-on or luxury. Funding agencies including CLIR, the National Endowment for the Humanities, and the National Historic Publications & Records Committee, which once excluded digitization, have revamped their programs to promote it. CLIR's Hidden Collections program now focuses on "Digitizing Hidden Special Collections and Archives."[4]

Growing interest in digitization is driven by several factors. Just as we reached a tipping point where it is broadly understood that access to information about collections will be online, "access" is rapidly coming to mean page images and searchable full-text.[5] In addition, preservation of digital files, another early problem, is being ensured by the growth of robust and trusted institutional, organizational, and disciplinary repositories. Globalization is also contributing to the shift toward digitization, motivating us to integrate our rare and unique holdings into a global cultural heritage. Finally—and perhaps most importantly for our consideration of the enduring value of special collections—digitizing special collections is transformative, allowing materials to be used for very different purposes than those intended by their authors as well as our predecessors. Researchers are combining descriptive bibliography, book history, and textual criticism with text-mining, geo-referencing, visualization, and linguistic analysis in ways that make "everything old...new again."

Library administrators have long found it useful to describe libraries as laboratories for the humanities to make the case that institutional funding for library collections, staff, and spaces is the equivalent of building, outfitting, and staffing state-of-the-art science labs. In this metaphor, collections are the "equipment" of the library-laboratory. Specialized subject librarians and curators build collections; work with library colleagues to ensure they are discoverable; and provide reference, instruction, outreach, and bibliographical services to facilitate and promote their use. Our work has typically ended at the reading room door, when the researcher begins hers. But digital scholarship relies on knowledge across different domains, and many libraries are establishing "Digital Humanities Laboratories" that promote collaboration and experimentation and bring together collections, hardware and software, and relevant expertise. Just as an "embedded librarian" provides specialized skills to a research team and becomes a full member of it, special collections and subject librarians, metadata librarians, and digital scholarship specialists provide essential expertise as part of research teams that form around library collections.[6]

In the introduction to *A New Republic of Letters: Memory and Scholarship in the Age of Digital Reproduction,* Jerome McGann makes a bold assertion: "Here is surely a truth now universally acknowledged: that the whole of our cultural inheritance has to be recurated and reedited in digital forms and institutional structures."[7]

McGann describes his methodology as follows: "I mean to...explore the mechanisms of both production history and transmission history and their complex, unfolding relations. In that analytic point of view, secondary documents–posthumous editions and transformation, for instance—are as important as the authorial manuscripts and early editions. So are all those attendant materials—reviews and commentaries—that expose and further define the character and meaning of the materials."[8] What he calls "secondary documents" are especially critical in the study of antiquity: "What memory would we have of the ancient world—of Sappho and Homer, for example—except for those secondary materials? None whatsoever."[9]

A University of Chicago project illustrates McGann's point and the potential for partnerships among scholars, students, librarians, and collectors. It began as a close study of individual editions and copies of printed books of works by Homer, with a focus on transmission, reception, and translation history. In a surprising twist, crowdsourcing and digital corpora solved a mystery that had eluded the team's efforts. Each approach drew on expertise from several disciplines and yielded new knowledge that only could have been created using their respective methods. The first resulted in a published collection catalog produced over six years by three librarians, three faculty members, two graduate students, and a collector; the second was a competition to identify marginalia in one volume that drew 50,000 online hits and took thirty-six hours to solve. Together they illustrate the complementarity of "bibliographical technologies" and the need to incorporate new methods into our research toolkit.

In 2007, Michael Lang donated his collection of 187 separate Homer editions (259 volumes) ranging from the fifteenth-century to the twentieth to the University of Chicago Library. In an essay he wrote for the collection catalog, Lang described two motivating factors in forming the collection. First, he wanted

> to apply, or at least test, the collector's belief regarding what one might call the "substance of format": that study of the physical printed book in which a text first appeared can add to one's understanding not only of the intentions of its author, editor, or publisher, but also of the impact that text had on its first readers.[10]

But he also acknowledged

> another species of "value"—an incalculable, impressionistic one that, at least in library budget requests, dares not speak its name: the one generated by the physical encounter between a student or scholar and

original materials. The benefit of such experience does not lend itself to clinical analysis, or even to lucid description. It is neither objective nor logical, and those who have not experienced it often dismiss it as foolish sentimentalism.[11]

Michael Lang chose the University of Chicago as the home for his collection because his vision for its future aligned with the University's strong classical tradition and core curriculum. Homer has been and remains required reading for first-year students since the inaugural year of classes in 1892. Among the most illustrious and influential publications commissioned by the University of Chicago Press, founded in 1890 as one of the University's main divisions to disseminate scholarship, is Richmond Lattimore's translation of *The Iliad,* published in 1949. In accepting the Lang gift, we made a commitment to continue building the collection by acquiring editions and translations that are not in the collection as well as newly published ones; and developing the collection in new directions, for example, graphic novels, works for children, and illustrated editions. We also agreed to produce a scholarly catalog of the collection to illustrate its research value. *Homer in Print; A Catalogue of the Bibliotheca Homerica Langiana at the University of Chicago Library,* edited by Glenn W. Most and Alice Schreyer (Chicago: The University of Chicago Library, 2013), fills a gap in the Homeric literature that Lang recognized as a collector: the lack of an in-depth study of printed editions of Homer's works. As it turned out, the project also allowed the donor to participate in the process by which the gift of a private collection to an academic institution contributes to graduate education as well as bibliographical research.

Our first task was to delineate the scope of the catalog and decide how best to tell the story of the production, distribution, and reception of the physical books. The Bibliotheca Homerica Langiana (BHL) is very strong in early and significant Greek editions and near-comprehensive for English translations. We decided that instead of complete bibliographical descriptions, we would highlight substantive copy-specific information such as provenance and marginalia and focus on the transmission of the text through editions and translations. Each item in the collection has its own entry and mini-essay, researched and written by a graduate student;

the volume also includes scholarly essays by two faculty members and Lang's reflections on building the collection.

Over the course of the work we identified and resolved several questions that illustrate interrelated strands of bibliographical inquiry. One was textual, the second a matter of eighteenth-century book trade practice, the third relates to the history of reading, and the most recent took us into the world of twentieth-century fine printing. The amount of time and effort devoted to investigating each puzzle is considerably disproportionate to the sentence that alludes to it in the catalog, but they are great examples of the opportunities for discovery that arise in such projects and how we functioned as a team to answer them.

Lang proposed that for the English translations, we transcribe the first lines of each edition of both *The Iliad* and *The Odyssey*. I confess that I did not at first recognize the value of this feature. But as soon as we began, I understood that they are the best way to convey the great variety of literary genres, language, meter, and syntax across the translations. The opening lines on the page thus form an essential part of the narrative entries, which explore the translator's theory of translation and editorial antecedents in order to present the rationale for producing yet another new translation.

Diana Moser, a PhD candidate in classics, researched and wrote the descriptions of the English translations, by far the largest group. While working on Pope's *Iliad*, she identified a rarely discussed revision that completely eclipsed an earlier version.

The first (1715) and second (1720) editions of Pope's *Iliad*, and a 1729 reprint, begin: "THE Wrath of *Peleus'* Son, the direful Spring/Of all the *Grecian* Woes, O Goddess, sing!" The opening lines of the third edition (1731–32) are, "Achilles' Wrath, to *Greece* the direful spring/ Of woes unnumber'd, heav'nly Goddess, sing!" This reading became the norm. David Vander Meulen at the University of Virginia pointed out a reference to the change in the introduction to Steven Shankman's 1996 Penguin edition of Pope's translation (Shankman dates the revision to the 1736 edition).[12] As Vander Meulen remarked, Shankman's translation—only available in paperback—is a reminder that collectors cannot ignore such unprepossessing editions.[13] Shankman notes that the revision may have been a response to criticism by John Dennis of Pope's phrase, "all the *Grecian* woes."[14] Pope seems to have adopted a reading close to that of Thomas Tickell's translation of Book 1, which also appeared in 1715: "Achilles' fatal Wrath, whence Discord rose,/That brought the Sons of *Greece* unnumber'd Woes." Samuel Johnson, in *The Lives of the Most Eminent English Poets,* remarks, "To compare the two translations would be tedious; the palm is now given universally to Pope; but I think the first lines of Tickell's were rather to be preferred, and Pope seems to have since borrowed something from them in the correction of his own."[15]

The second investigation came up in one of the catalog essays, "Quarrelling over Homer in France and England, 1711–1715."[16] David Wray looks at the "Homer Quarrel," a skirmish in the Battle of the Ancients and Moderns. Mme. Anne Dacier's literal, prose translation of the *Iliad* into French appeared in 1711 in the popular three-volume novel format. David Wray compares her translation of the Proem to several others, including that of John Ozell, who translated her prose back into English the following year.[17] Wray quoted a passage in verse which, during copyediting, we discovered was printed as prose in the original. In response to a query, Wray explained that he had not transcribed it as it appears in the first edition because Ozell and all of his contemporaries understood it to be a blank-verse translation. In his preface, Ozell praises Dacier's translation, but then expresses doubt "whether an English translation of Homer, any otherwise than in verse, can be made so as to please an English reader." Later he asserts that "in all translations, regard ought to [be] had, not only to the sense of the original, but to the very manner of the composition, which ought to be resembled as near as possible, and not a new one introduced." Wray is convinced that Lintot printed the work as prose simply to save paper. Of course, we kept the blank-verse form in his essay and included this explanation for the discrepancy.[18] Happily, David Wray is contemplating producing the first-ever edition of Ozell's translation printed, as he intended it to be, in blank verse.

One question hovered over the entire project and was not solved until after the publication of the catalog. Ever since he purchased his copy of the Aldine 1504 edition of Homer's *Odyssey*, Michael Lang was intrigued by the script used for extensive handwritten annotations in the second volume. Over the years we worked on the project, University of Chicago linguists from several departments examined the script and declared it "not Georgian," "not Turkish," "not Armenian," and definitely not Greek. Randall McLeod, a book historian from the University of Toronto, was confident it was a form of nineteenth-century shorthand, but no one was able to take it any further.[19] Lang was determined not to give up. As the project was winding down—catalog published, scholarly colloquium and exhibition behind us—he offered to sponsor a $1000 prize to the first person to identify the script, provide evidence to support the conclusion, and execute a translation of selected portions of the mysterious marginalia.

We posted images of two pages with dense annotations on our website and—quite naively, in retrospect—provided information on how to examine the book in our reading room. Of course we were immediately flooded with requests for high-resolution images of all the pages with annotations, which we did immediately. News of the contest started spreading online, especially after it was picked up by the social media site Reddit and became a global news story. Within thirty-six hours we had a winner and two runners-up, all of whom arrived at the same conclusion.[20]

The winner was Daniele Metilli, an Italian computer engineer and software developer in Milan who is currently enrolled in a digital humanities course and training for a career in libraries and archives. Working with Giula Accetta, a colleague who is proficient in contemporary Italian stenography and fluent in French, Metilli identified the mystery script as the French system of tachygraphy invented by Jean Coulon de Thévénot in the late eighteenth century. Vanya Visnjic, a PhD student in classics at Princeton University with an interest in cryptography, was the second contestant to identify the script and provide translations, as did Gallagher Flinn, a PhD student in linguistics at the University of Chicago.

Based on the mix of French words with the script and a legible date of April 25, 1854, the Italian team concluded, as had MacLeod, that it was a system of French stenography in use in the mid-nineteenth century. They examined French nineteenth-century stenography manuals on Google Books and found a chart comparing one of them to Jean Coulon de Thévenot's "tachygraphie" system published in 1789. Using an 1819 edition of Thévenot's work, revised by a professor of stenography, N. Patey, and armed with two contemporary French translations of the *Odyssey*—one published in 1842, the other in 1854–66—they began to translate the marginalia.

80

In Thévenot's system, inspired by the shorthand system of Tironian notes that are said to have been invented by Cicero's scribe and used into the Middle Ages, "every consonant and vowel has a starting shape, and they combine together to form new shapes representing syllables," Metilli explained.[21] "The vertical alignment is especially important, as the position of a letter above or below the line, or even the length of a letter segment can change the value of the grapheme. This explains why most notes in the *Odyssey* shorthand are underlined, the line being key to the transcription."[22]

Recently I met a collector of T. E. Lawrence. When I mentioned the BHL copy of the 1932 Bruce Rogers edition of Lawrence's translation of the *Odyssey*, considered by Joseph Blumenthal and others to be the most beautiful book produced by the twentieth-century private press movement, he asked if our copy smells. After I recovered from my surprise, he explained that the special ink used in the book gives off a distinct smell. We have two copies. They both have a peppery aroma, distinct even when the book is closed, and it is stronger in the copy in finer condition. The ink is made from oil of copaiba, popular today as one of the cure-all "essential oils." We know that the smell of individual copies of books provide evidence of the conditions in which they were read. Here is one physical characteristic of an entire edition that is unlikely—though not, of course, impossible—to be reproduced online.

In his essay on forming the BHL, Michael Lang observes that

> those engaged in critical analysis or serious scholarship are not immune to sensations of affinity arising from a physical connection with the subject of their study, and it is naïve to discount the subtle effects of such sensations. On the other hand, it is equally naïve to believe that university libraries should operate on romantic principles, plunking down hard cash to acquire original material in the hope that exposure will inspire and promote a greater quality of scholarship than might otherwise be the case. Here is where the private collector, able to act in support of intangible benefits, can play a useful role.[23]

"The private collector, able to act in support of intangible benefits, can play a useful role." What practical wisdom and generosity of spirit are embodied in these words. As part of the desire for accountability in higher education, university administrators are eager for data that documents impact. We need to remember that discoveries are often the result of "intangible benefits." By their very nature, rare books, manuscripts, and archives, the sources on which original research depends, do not reveal their secrets at first glance. Gifts of these materials from private collectors are essential to the ability of special collections to support research.

Social media and electronic resources made it possible for Metilli "to identify the shorthand and translate the first fragments in a few hours on a Thursday night.... If I didn't have access to online sources such as Google Books, the Greek Word Study Tool of the Perseus Digital Library, and the French corpora of the National Center for Textual and Lexical Resources, I probably wouldn't have won. What great times we live in!"[24]

At the beginning of the twenty-first century, library directors were concerned about succession planning for special collections. Many curators and special collections directors were approaching retirement age and, based on recent searches, the directors were unsure where the next generation would come from. The anticipated "crisis" never materialized, and the profession is flourishing. Early-career librarians and recent PhDs are drawn to careers in special collections librarianship, seeking out training and professional development at venues that have become more robust, responsive, and accessible, including library schools, continuing education programs, and professional organizations.

Several benchmarks document this trend. In 2004 the RBMS preconference in New Haven attracted 301 attendees. Attendance always varies somewhat depending on location, although the 2009 preconference in Charlottesville, a location not known for being easy to reach, drew 412 for the organization's celebratory fiftieth anniversary. The 2014 conference in Las Vegas was attended by 436 individuals.

Rare Book School at the University of Virginia has grown dramatically. In 2004, 337 students attended classes; in 2014, the number was 424. Over the same decade thirty-nine new courses were introduced (with another eight to be launched in 2015).[25] The School is expanding beyond Charlottesville to enable year-round programming and to make it possible to offer courses in specialized topics at institutions with first-class collections of relevant primary materials. Rare Book School relies on learning by handling and close examination of "the stuff." This approach gives adult learners the same excitement and engagement—those "intangible benefits" that fuel research—as undergraduate and graduate students experience when they use special collections materials in their courses.

RBMS and RBS offer scholarship support for those interested in special collections librarianship and for librarians who want to develop their bibliographical expertise. The Institute for Museum and Library Studies (IMLS) funded an IMLS-RBS fellowship program for early-career professionals with a "demonstrable interest" in special collections librarianship, with funding for attending RBMS and RBS.

Daniele Metilli summed it up perfectly in his statement that the Homer contest confirmed his desire to work in libraries or archives: "Where else would I find such wonderful mysteries to solve?"[26] There is no end to the mysteries hidden in the pages of rare books that await new readers who will ask new questions. Collectors, curators, librarians, archivists, conservators, students, scholars, teachers, and booksellers strive to pass this ongoing process of inquiry, discovery, and learning on to coming generations. For them as for us, "everything old is new again."

NOTES

1. Peter Allen and Carole Bayer Sager, *Continental American*, A & M Records SP3643, 1974, 33 rpm.
2. Authors Guild v. HathiTrust, 755 F. 3d 87 (2d Cir. 2014) at 10:19, Association of Research Libraries, www.arl.org/storage/documents/publications/agvhathitrust-decision-jun2014.pdf.
3. Jonathan Band, "What Does the *HATHITRUST* Decision Mean for Libraries?" Library Copyright Alliance, July 7, 2014, p. 4, www.librarycopyrightalliance.org/storage/documents/article-hathitrust-analysis-7ju12014.pdf.
4. "Digitizing Hidden Special Collections and Archives," Council on Information and Library Resources, www.clir.org/fellowships/hiddencollections.
5. "Hidden Collection, Scholarly Barriers: Creating Access to Unprocessed Special Collections Materials in North American's Research Libraries," White Paper for the Association of Research Libraries Task Force on Special Collections, compiled by Barbara M. Jones (June 6, 2013), p. 4, Association of Research Libraries, www.arl.org/storage/documents/publications/hidden-colls-white-paper-jun03.pdf.
6. David Shumaker, *The Embedded Librarians,* abstract, *Online* 36, no. 4 (July/August 2012), http://proxy.uchicago.edu/login?url=http://search.ebscohost.com.proxy.uchicago.edu/login.aspx?direct=true&db=c9h&AN=78235097&site=eds-live&scope=site.

7. Jerome McGann, *A New Republic of Letters* (Cambridge, Mass.: Harvard University Press, 2014), 1.
8. Ibid., 8.
9. Ibid.
10. M. C. Lang, "The Architecture of Accumulation: A Book Collector's Apology," in *Homer in Print: A Catalogue of the Bibliotheca Homerica Langiana at the University of Chicago Library,* ed. Glenn W. Most and Alice Schreyer (Chicago: The University of Chicago Library, 2013), 3.
11. Ibid., 5.
12. *The Iliad of Homer,* trans. Alexander Pope, ed. Steven Shankman (London: Penguin Books, 1996), xviii; David Vander Meulen, email message to author, May 30, 2012.
13. Vander Meulen, Ibid.
14. Shankman, xviii.
15. Samuel Johnson, *The Lives of the Most Eminent English Poets,* vol. 3 (London: Printed for C. Bathurst, 1781), 177–78, http://find.galegroup.com/ecco/infomark.do?&source=gale&prodId=ECCO&userGroupName=chic_rbw&tabID=T001&docId=CW3312652643&type=multipage&contentSet=ECCOArticles&version=1.0&docLevel=FASCIMILE.
16. David Wray, "Quarrelling over Homer in France and England, 1711–1715," in *Homer in Print,* 300–31.
17. Ibid., 309.
18. Ibid., 330, endnote 11.
19. Randall McLeod, email message to author, March 8, 2012.
20. "Homer Mystery Script Contest Winner and Results," The University of Chicago Library News, May 5, 2014, http://news.lib.uchicago.edu/blog/2014/05/05/homer-mystery-script-contest-winner-and-results/.
21. Daniele Metilli, "French Tachygraphic Notes in a 1504 copy of Homer's *Odyssey,*" 8, http://metilli.com/files/Metilli-Odyssey-2014-05-05.pdf.
22. Ibid.
23. Lang, "Architecture of Accumulation," 5–6.
24. Daniele Metilli, email message to author, March 30, 2014.
25. Amanda Nelsen, email message to author, June 26, 2015.
26. Daniele Metilli, email message to author, March 29, 2014.

CHAPTER 10

Special Collections and the Booksellers of Today

TOM CONGALTON

First of all I'd like to whine a little bit about the topic of the panel on which I was invited to speak for the colloquium that inspired this book, "Special Collections in an Age of Digital Scholarship." I'm not from your world. I'm just a simple bookseller from out of the past. When it comes to talking about special collections in a digital era, I might seem like an odd choice. In 1969 I went to work shelving books at the Monmouth County Library in Freehold, New Jersey. While I was there I was surprised to see how quick librarians were to embrace then new library technologies such as the fax machine transmissions that took twenty minutes to reproduce a single page, microfilming of periodicals, the use of keypunch machines for cataloging, and similar modern wonders.

Obviously this openness to, and emphasis on embracing new technology, sometimes to what seemed like the detriment of physical books, has continued for nearly half a century and has turned out to be invaluable preparation in our digital age. Thus librarians in general seem like they are well situated to deal with challenges in a digital age. Most booksellers, on the other hand, are pretty much only interested in expanding their grasp of technology insomuch as it positively impacts their bottom line. This recalls a yearlong, on-again, off-again conversation I had with Ken Lopez in the mid-1980s about whether or not I needed a computer for my business. Ken, who used to be a programmer and whom I was asking for guidance, came down strongly on the side of "whatever."

I guess my point is that booksellers who deal with institutions in the digital age are not ourselves particularly well prepared for that era, and will have to take our cues from librarians. We are unlikely to give librarians what they need unless librarians tell us what that is. From my point of view, what little interaction that I've had with digital materials has had to do with the manuscripts and emails of living authors, both in harvesting them and in some cases appraising them, and in every case these events have been fraught with practical problems with which I've been ill-equipped to deal. Obviously booksellers will have to, and are learning, but librarians will have to guide us in how we can serve their needs.

However, where I think that booksellers can immediately contribute to the future of library collections is by doing what we have always done, acting as the hunter-gatherers or truffle hounds for material, and especially previously neglected material, often in nontraditional formats, for special collections.

This may be a little off-point, but the course I co-teach at Rare Book School in Virginia, called Developing Collections: Donors, Librarians and Booksellers, has a certain emphasis on nonbook material such as ephemera, photography, obsolete audio and visual formats, and similar artefacts, both printed and otherwise.

One of our students, a graduate student in a nonlibrary field, after having spent most of a week handling 7" vinyl records, old cassette tapes of early genre music performances, vernacular photography collections, London prostitute cards, printed cloth broadsides, and other similarly nonbook examples that we used in class, observed that these objects, for her at least, served as a sort of "gateway drug" into special collections and the books and manuscripts that have been more traditionally accumulated there. I believe she referred to the material as "crack for book people."

The beauty of book collecting is that it pretty much includes any possible topic of interest to human beings. If you are interested in anything in the world there are probably books about it, and as such, our mission as booksellers, librarians, or collectors is pretty much unlimited. We make the rules. Increasingly it seems like our futures are going to encompass nonbook materials.

This obviously will have repercussions not only on what we pursue, and how we preserve it, digitally or otherwise, but also on how we view ourselves. When do curators of special collections morph into museum curators, or when do booksellers become antique dealers? We're going to have to confront these questions in the relatively near future.

It seems to me that our cultural influences (and especially the influences on youth culture—by which I mean anyone who is younger than I am) have become increasingly visually oriented. We will have to determine how these more visual materials lend themselves to digital preservation.

By this I don't mean that our constituents are only attracted to pretty pictures, but I think that it does mean we are going to have to look for ways to integrate nonbook artefactual material into special collections as part of a strategy of interactive outreach. We need to lure students, scholars, and members of the general public into libraries to look at those pretty pictures in order to induce them into further exploring the textual and artefactual richness of the existing books and manuscripts within our collections.

I think that all stripes of collectors—and we are all collectors—will find opportunities in this. Strictly from my own point of view, it's always an advantage to find a way to expand the parameters of an existing collection, and there will be financial rewards for booksellers to do this, and there will be both professional and creative rewards for librarians who develop and, dare I say, "market" unusual collections in neglected fields and formats to their constituents.

It is in the nature of my chosen profession, that after every talk in the colloquium I wanted to stand up and ask each one of the speakers, "What can I sell you in the future?" Obviously, this is self-serving, but it is also a valid question. I'm perfectly willing to be self-serving, but how can we as booksellers serve librarians in the future?

By the way, this isn't a rhetorical question. I want answers.

One other observation I'd like to make is that in all the serious and admittedly important conversations that occurred during the colloquium, there was little mention of the sense of fun that we are all so frequently a part of. For me, at least, and I suspect for many of you, every day is an adventure, and every day is a treasure hunt. If we can convey our enthusiasm for the material that we pursue and preserve, I suspect we will have far fewer anxieties about the future of the book, and of special collections. Jay Satterfield touches on this with his theory of "exuberant chaos" described in his contribution to this book (see chapter 14).

I'll finish my brief essay with an anecdote that illustrates the existential dilemmas that face the modern rare bookseller. I'll call it "The Case of the Willa Cather Box."

A few years ago I was at a book fair in Lawrenceville, New Jersey, and another dealer was offering, suitably ensconced in a glass case, a cardboard box—an empty cardboard box. It attracted me because it had a really nice label from the publisher Alfred A. Knopf, and it was addressed to Willa Cather. The postmark was very clear, so you could read it and it gave you a hint about what might have been in it.

So I spent a couple or three hundred dollars to buy this box.

The first thing I had to do, because it was really fragile, was take it to a bookbinder, who happened to also be set up at the book fair, and immediately commissioned a folding box to put my empty box in. I think there's probably some sort of important Zen lesson in there that I'm just not smart enough to understand.

So that took a month. But I finally got my box back, and then, like Cinderella and the glass slipper, I had to very carefully audition books to see what might have fit in the box. I finally figured it out, or at least I think I figured out, that it was two copies of the illustrated edition of "Death Comes for the Archbishop."

Then, armed with all of this knowledge, I called an institutional librarian and said, "I want to sell you this empty box for $950!" He said, "That's ridiculous, we don't want an empty box addressed to Willa Cather!" But what they really meant, and finally actually did say, was, "We don't collect artifacts."

Now, I'm pretty sure that at that exact moment the librarian was standing next to a glass case that held the typewriter, pipes, and underpants of a Very Famous Writer. So I said "Yes, you do! You're standing next to a case that has the typewriter of a Very Famous Writer!"

But he wasn't buying it.

Anyway, eventually I was able to manage to sell it to another institutional library where somebody is probably going to have to digitally preserve that empty box. And somebody's going to have to tell me how they do that.

CHAPTER 11

Acknowledging the Past

DANIEL DE SIMONE

The topic of the panel at the colloquium of which I originally was a part had been asked to consider these questions about library special collections: what has endured, what has changed, and what may not endure in the future? These are large questions and this chapter is an effort to begin a conversation with you the reader that will generate some answers, rather than simply to present a tidy list of observations that would inevitably be incomplete and potentially unsatisfactory. I will examine the first two questions, but twist the third to reflect what we can do as a community of librarians, collectors, and booksellers to acknowledge what is right and good, and how we might adapt to what has changed.

As so many of us are taught, libraries have traditionally exercised three main functions: to collect, preserve, and create access to the materials under their care. On a university campus like Case Western Reserve University, they offer these services to faculty and students and to the public through exhibitions, programs, and research support. Public libraries, many of which have special collections departments, have more interaction with the general public. In addition to the services listed above, public libraries may provide language training, help with job applications, and in many cases provide a safe haven for children of working parents and for adults down on their luck. While public libraries have taken on more and more social service responsibilities, their special collections departments are transforming themselves in the manner in which they accommodate digital research methods and the savvy patrons who require better tools and collaborative spaces in which to work.

When I was in graduate school, I was part of a growing number of humanities students who were trained to study history through a conceptual perspective. The conceptualization of history allowed for a multiplicity of ways that events could be understood. Cultural and gender studies, such as African-American history, environmental history, women's history, Native American studies, blossomed and new academic specialties were born as the humanities grew to meet the demands of the "new history." Special collection libraries began buying books to satisfy the needs of the department, and a new generation of booksellers, many trained in these academic programs, built inventories to fill this demand. For the book trade this created new markets, driven by both libraries and private collectors. Forty years later, it is happening again. With digital texts online, the demand is now for annotated texts, ephemera, and manuscripts, and the book market is again being transformed. Inventories around the globe reflect this transition and the questions for the future are, can the market sustain this demand, and what will be next?

In conversations with members of the book collecting community, the consensus seems to be that not only are books becoming scarcer and much, much more expensive, but collectors are themselves getting older. A look at the demographic of collectors who are members in the Grolier Club, Rowfant Club, Caxton Club, Book Club of California, etc., seems to accentuate this point. "Where are the younger book collectors?" is a refrain often heard from the bookseller, collector, and librarian communities. After years of buying books and building their collections, many collectors find themselves filling in with the odd book and perhaps finding a manuscript or an upgrade that they can add to their collections. The value of books has also made it more difficult to continue buying, especially in fields where they used to be plentiful but have now become mainstream subject areas taken up by institutions and part of library collection development policies. Other collectors are focusing more and more on materials that have unique or distinguished characteristics and qualities that "add value" to a book or manuscript.

After nearly forty years working with rare books, I have witnessed the many transitions that have taken place in our world. All of us, in one way or another, have encountered the change that is affecting the rare book world as we know it. We are experiencing it in different ways, but recognizing these changes is part of what unites us. Booksellers, collectors, and librarians have a bond with deep roots, forged over many generations. Without a doubt this is the most enduring characteristic of our interconnected lives. The International League of Antiquarian Booksellers (ILAB) carries as its motto "the love of books unites us." This I think is true, and it is what makes me most optimistic about the future.

At the 2014 Case Western Reserve University colloquium and at the Library of Congress "Symposium on Authenticity of Print Materials" in Washington, DC, the year before, every seat was filled. You could feel a sense of excitement in the air among the collectors, booksellers, and librarians in attendance. This is not an uncommon phenomenon when our tribes meet. For those of us who teach, in my case at the Colorado Book Seminar, these seats are filled with booksellers, librarians, and collectors eager to learn about the book and the traditions that have fostered it. The same goes for Rare Book School, and some of the MLS programs around the country that teach courses in rare books and special collections.

Go to the opening night of a book fair. Witness, as I have for decades, the obvious synergy that is created over a book or manuscript. See the private collector acting as buyer and in some cases as teacher to the bookseller. Watch the librarian examining a text or an image for its appropriateness for her collection. Feel the excitement of the bookseller when he meets a new customer or passes a book to an established client that was purchased with her in mind.

Enthusiasm for rare books is infectious. For me what is most enduring in our world of rare books is the interdependent nature of our relationships, which are based on two of the most perfect objects ever conceived by mankind: the codex manuscript and the printed book.

Given this insight, I think that it is incumbent on us to figure out new ways of spreading the gospel of the book, to demonstrate for new audiences the opportunities that are part of the world of rare books. The fact is we know that when people are exposed to rare materials they are not only challenged intellectually but also experientially as they take possession and handle the physical manifestation of a thought or idea. What they encounter is the book, the manuscript, or the piece of printed ephemera that carries with it information about its manufacture, use, ownership, and history. I believe it is this combination that stimulates the excitement with which we are all so familiar.

How do we create opportunities to spread the word? How do we identify a new audience? How do we communicate our enthusiasm for the physical object to a younger, more diverse, technically sophisticated group of people? Most importantly, how do librarians, booksellers, and private collectors work together to accomplish this goal? This is the very issue that has occupied so much of my time since beginning my job as Librarian at the Folger Shakespeare Library. It has caused me to understand better the nature of our existing audience and to speak with other librarians and museum directors to learn more about how they are dealing with the issue. I can tell you that my search for information about "audience" building has led to the realization that although it is much talked about, this is a topic that is neither well studied nor written about—especially as it relates to the book world. There is a sense that to grow beyond our present circumstance we must think about turning the casual visitor into a friend for life. Institutions that reach out to the public through exhibitions and programming must come up with new ways to communicate what we know about our collections. Institutions must begin to have conversations among themselves with the aim of creating a new pedagogy that will translate for visitors what we know about the meaning and nuance of historical materials and how they can enhance their lives. This is a challenge that cannot wait. It demands that the best minds in museums, libraries, the book trade, and the collecting world work together to tackle this issue and make it a priority for the future.

When it comes to the book trade, the issue of creating new audience is equally important. I have been repeating for over a decade the mantra that one of the best markets in the country is the library market. In most cases, institutions have annual budgets and collection development policies that outline for the trade the current and developing collecting paths. For the bookseller, this offers an opportunity to develop deeper relationships with the rare book librarians who control budgets now, and to plant seeds for those librarians who will come to these positions in the future. I have suggested elsewhere that booksellers should follow the example of the library world and begin a program of summer internships with library students. If booksellers want future librarians to understand what exactly booksellers do, how they do it, and the stresses that come with running a business, then they should invite them to work in their shops. Not as a packer but as a personal assistant. Show them how the operations of the book business works, take them to an auction or on a scouting trip, get them involved in producing a catalog—and pay them a salary for their work. If ten booksellers were to do this over the next five years, there would be fifty young librarians ready to enter the world of special collections not only with bibliographical knowledge, but also, and most importantly for the book trade, an understanding of how the book business operates.

In October 2014, an exhibition opened at the University of Dayton which contained highlights from the collection of Stuart Rose. Stuart is one of America's most preeminent collectors, and he allowed the library to pick fifty items from his library and put them on display at the entrance to the University Library. The opportunity loomed so large for the library staff that they enlisted the help of the humanities and science faculties and encouraged them to make the choices from the Rose Collection and to write item descriptions of books they thought best represented their own research. A catalog of the exhibition, *Imprints and Impressions: Milestones in Human Progress*, was published[1] for the opening of the exhibition in September 2014. The faculty also committed to assigning projects that required their students to use the rare book collections and to relate their research to the exhibition. In effect, nearly the entire undergraduate population was exposed in one way or another to historical materials from the Rose Collection. According to the University of Dayton library administration, most of these students had never worked with rare materials before, and most had never visited the Special Collections Department in the library.

Another collector, Michael Lang, made a gift of his collection of the works of Homer to the University of Chicago, with the proviso that the collection be used by the Classics Department as a tool for teaching. Faculty and graduate students wrote both historical and bibliographical descriptions of the collection and published a catalog, *Bibliotheca Homerica Langiana*,[2] which was issued in 2013. The Classics Department embraced the collection and organized course work for both graduate and undergraduate students that required use of the historical collections.

In both of these examples, private collectors teamed up with special collections librarians, faculty, and students to create opportunities to expand the audience for rare materials. They ensured that their collections, formed with a passion for both the content and the historical object, would be used to inspire others to learn and to enjoy the importance of the printed book and manuscript.

I don't have answers, just questions. My hope is that as a community, we can agree that an opportunity exists to address issues that are inescapable as the world of rare books changes. I hope that my comments will inspire many others in the profession to pick up this thread, build upon it, and communicate new ideas that will help us endure through the generations to come.

ACKNOWLEDGMENTS

I would like to thank Joel Silver and the organizers of "Acknowledging the Past, Forging the Future: A National Colloquium on Library Special Collections," which inspired this chapter. I would especially like to recognize Bob Jackson, who over a decade ago initiated a dialogue with me about the relationship between the librarian and the private collector. This conversation developed into a program at the Library of Congress which included booksellers as well as collectors and librarians. I was gratified to be a part of the 2014 colloquium program that he was so instrumental in putting together. I would also like to thank Arnold Hirshon for making everyone so welcome here in Cleveland and on the campus of Case Western Reserve University.

NOTES

1. A list of items in the exhibit and commentary about each item can be found at http://ecommons.udayton.edu/rosebk_commentary/.
2. Glenn W. Most, Alice D. Schreyer, M. C. Lang, and David Wray, *Homer in Print: A Catalogue of the Bibliotheca Homerica Langiana at the University of Chicago Library* (Chicago: The University of Chicago Library, 2013).

CHAPTER 12

Literary Archives

How They Have Changed and How
They Are Changing

KEN LOPEZ

I have been a bookseller for about forty years, and have been dealing primarily in modern literary first editions and living writers' literary archives since the early 1990s. Over the years things have changed in a number of ways, and they continue to do so, with digitization being one major factor.

Acknowledging and exploring the past is a big part of what preserving literary archives is about. It is worth taking note of the significant changes to these archives in recent years, and the implications of those changes going forward.

One of the first and most visible changes is that writers' literary archives today seldom include the kind of cut-and-paste manuscripts that used to be prevalent in the past. In earlier archives, the author would write a draft and then revise it by literally cutting-and-pasting the revisions onto the original sheet of paper to save having to retype the entire thing. Those manuscripts showed the physical evidence of the author reworking it, trying to improve it, and trying to get it right. You could see the archaeology of the work by looking at a single draft with its corrections, additions, and changes.

In those earlier archives, you would get one or two heavily annotated drafts that yielded significant information about the process of writing the work; today you do not see this very much. What you tend to see is a lot of paper, because it is very easy to press the "print" key and get a whole new, clean typescript. A single book will be a half a dozen, a dozen, sometimes three boxes full of manuscripts, all for the same title, all with very slight changes, but that make it very difficult to collate and understand the process of the creation of the work—even if you also possess the digital versions of them. The evolution of a writer's work was easy and self-evident in a literary archive before, but now, especially given digitization, it can be hard to do that; even digital files leave changes unmarked in the final digital files that are retained.

There are other things that used to appear regularly in archives that are also increasingly uncommon now. One group—seemingly slight or trivial—are the ephemeral items, such as brochures and marketing materials. For example, for this colloquium, until I arrived here I had seen nothing on paper today; previously, all of the information, advertising, and promotional material had been distributed via email and the website. This is a boon for the trees that were not sacrificed to make paper promotional materials, but there's a downside to it as well. A few years ago I was dealing with a writer's archive that was large and that a couple of librarians were coming to see. We—the writer and I—realized belatedly that we had forgotten about a group of boxes in her garage. We had literally hundreds of boxes that we had prepared to show the librarians—but then there was this other group in the garage. Concerned that we would overwhelm the librarians with the sheer quantity of material, much of it ephemeral printed matter that we thought was all junk, we quickly went out to clean it up, that is to get the good stuff and save it, and get rid of the trash. The writer and I went out to the garage and started pulling out all the various marketing materials for writers' workshops and other such items that tend to accumulate in an active writer's life. We were throwing them away so that what would be left was a high percentage of original, unique material.

We thought we were doing a very good thing for the librarians who were coming by winnowing out the junk and saving the unique, original, creative materials. When the librarians arrived, we told them what we had done. They were aghast. What the writer and I didn't think about, but that the librarians did, was that these brochures about these events, these marketing materials, might in a hundred years from now be the only information, the only evidence, that such events had ever taken place. These unique materials had value, and to have discarded them would have been a significant loss.

In this respect, archives are mosaics. Each piece within the archive represents a single piece of the mosaic. Once combined, they begin to create a picture that is understandable and conveys some meaning and information. Archives are never absolutely complete, but still they create a picture that can't be assembled otherwise. It is important to preserve them to recognize, and in some ways reconstruct, something from the past that is understood to be of value and worth preserving. Even something as seemingly mundane and trivial as marketing materials can add to our understanding and knowledge of the time and milieu in which they were created.

Correspondence is another element that has changed since I first started dealing in archives over forty years ago. Everyone knows that in the past archives contained many letters. Nowadays the letters that most often remain in an archive tend to be form letters or formal letters. Personal communications are more likely to take the form of emails, telephone calls, texts, or social media postings. I was recently working on an archive that had a group of letters from a writer to his wife written while he was at a months-long writing workshop in the early 1960s. He told her about the informal Thursday night readings that the writers in the workshop were holding for each other. It turned out that these Thursday night readings became Thursday night parties, lubricated with alcohol. Soon, somebody brought marijuana and turned it into Thursday night pot parties. Before too long, somebody found out about LSD, and they turned into Thursday night LSD parties (and this was when LSD was still legal).

The writer who hosted these parties was Ken Kesey, who was at the Stanford writing program at the time. After he graduated from the writing program he took the concept that these readings had developed into—the free-form LSD parties—and called them the Acid Tests, which he turned into a series of these events around the San Francisco Bay Area. Those acid tests evolved into what became the communal events of the counterculture: the large, free rock concerts where LSD was distributed freely (but by then it was illegal). The concerts took place in Golden Gate Park, and later migrated elsewhere, with the most famous one being the Woodstock music festival. The mythologist Joseph Campbell referred to them as the shared ecstatic communal experiences of this culture. Contained in the archive of this writer's letters was the description of the beginning of the process that resulted in Woodstock. Without tangible, archivable correspondence, I would not have known—no one would have known—that Woodstock grew out of a small group of writers' informal readings on Thursday night in the Stanford writing program.

Almost every archive I have encountered has had a random or miscellaneous group of photographs, sometimes a handful, sometimes hundreds, sometimes thousands. A recent archive I sold was about two-thirds digital. This made the photos harder to find because they weren't printed and lying around in boxes. They had resided on different machines over the years, and were preserved in different ways by the writer. It occurred to me to wonder what would have happened if this writer had died before transferring the digital archives. Today, much digital storage of personal materials is moving from residing on one's own personal computer, iPad, or smartphone and into the so-called "cloud." If this writer had died we would be left wondering, "Did he have cloud storage somewhere? Are there thousands of photographs somewhere that not only have no physical presence but can't be located digitally here in this house?" You would have to know about the existence of an account, or more than one. You would have to know the writer's passwords, and you would have to know that these things *existed* for you to be able to find them. You would have to know all of this before the account was cancelled because the writer had not paid the bill for storage, and all the digital items contained were erased. These digital materials stand at risk of getting lost at this moment in time in a way that they didn't when they had a primarily physical manifestation.

One of my customers, a collector, was a John Updike scholar who ran a John Updike website for many years. It was full of bibliographic information, photos, gossip, and contained a forum where other interested people could communicate with each other, ask and answer questions, make comments, and share their information and opinions. One day this collector's Internet service provider simply shut down. It was a small business up in Maine run by a couple of young guys. Apparently the increasingly competitive Internet business was squeezed to the point where they couldn't make a profit, so the owners simply unplugged the machines and shut down the business. My customer called them up and asked if he could at least retrieve his material from their servers and they essentially told him they didn't have time for him. Without having any backup, he lost ten years' worth of work that he had put in and that others had put in about John Updike. It just disappeared overnight, in cyberspace one day and out of existence the next.

There are numerous dangers to the archival environment in which we live when we rely so entirely on non-physical materials. Another recent archive with which I have been dealing has a large digital component. The writer asked, "Do you think they really want my honorary degrees? Do you think anybody's going to actually look at them? Do you think maybe I should just send a scan of them?" I said, "I think they do want them." I told him that the whole point of these archives was to preserve the original items—the "Thing Itself," not some representation of it. By analogy, in a magazine article I read recently, the rock-and-roll musician Neil Young compared the digital music we listen to on iPods and MP3s to looking at a photo of the painting of the Mona Lisa as opposed to looking at the painting itself. I was thinking this was the same thing. I told this writer, "You are getting paid a lot of money for this archive: they want the archive, they don't want pictures of the archive." So he began to understand.

What this exchange did for me was a little surprising. It made me realize—or ask the question—what is the Thing Itself that is being preserved here? I realized when I was talking to him that an image of an honorary degree is definitely not the same as an honorary degree, but the honorary degree itself was not the Thing Itself either; it was a representation of an honor that this institution was according to the writer. In some sense it was as much a pale shadow of the Thing Itself as the picture of the degree was of the degree. What I started to consider was that in this case the Thing Itself was an honor, an acknowledgment and indication of respect for the writer's work. However, "honor" and "respect" are intangibles. You cannot frame them or hang them on the wall, nor can you put them in a box and store them. They're part of what the poet Charles Olson called the "human universe."[1] Similarly, a printed book, or the manuscript of a printed book, is not ultimately the Thing Itself, but only something that points to the Thing Itself.

A book matters, and its manuscript may be preserved and valued because of the ideas it contains, the perceptions it reveals, the insight it yields, the wisdom it shows. It affects us because it enlightens us, broadens our understanding, widens our gaze, and elevates us as thinking and feeling living creatures. All of these things—wisdom, insight, understanding, perspective—are intangibles, but they are still the Things Themselves. They make up not only the "human universe," but also what the theologian Teilhard de Chardin called the "Noosphere,"[2] that is the mental, emotional, spiritual correlate to the physical atmosphere that surrounds us at all times, in which we live in and breathe, and to which our own thoughts and actions contribute.

Intangibles are what define us as human beings. They are what will endure. If we think of ourselves as merely preserving (or, in my case, selling) paper products, then our jobs may end in the near future as nearly everything is digitized (or at least we may be reduced to triviality or irrelevancy). However, if we think of ourselves as stewards who recognize and preserve that which elevates us as humans—and that improves ourselves, our culture, humanity in general, or the earth at large—then our task will endure, even as the archives take on new forms. It is an honor and a privilege to be a part of the process of acknowledging, and thus preserving, the Thing Itself—that which ultimately has value and meaning.

NOTES

1. Charles Olson, *Human Universe* (New York: Grove Press, 1958).
2. Pierre Teilhard de Chardin, *The Vision of the Past* (New York: Harper & Row, 1966), 71, 230, 261.

CHAPTER 13

Objects of Study

Special Collections in an Age of Digital Scholarship

STEPHEN ENNISS

In 1794 Samuel Ireland announced the discovery of a trove of Shakespeare letters and manuscripts, including what he claimed was the original manuscript of *King Lear*. The public interest in the discovery was so great that tickets had to be distributed to manage the number of people that wished to crowd into Ireland's home to see the papers. Hearing of the discovery, the diarist James Boswell joined the crowds, and, upon seeing the manuscript, is said to have kissed it and then remarked, "I shall now die contented, since I have lived to witness the present day."[1] Boswell apparently meant it; he was dead within a few weeks.

The Ireland forgeries, as they are now known, were only exposed as fakes when the forger, Samuel Ireland's own son, William, tried to pass off an entire play of his own fabrication as a newly discovered work by Shakespeare. Plans were made to produce *Vortigern and Rowena* at London's Drury Lane Theatre, but on opening night the audience saw through the obvious fraud and disrupted the performance with derisive laughter. The disturbance was so great the actors were unable to go on.

I am interested in the Ireland forgeries not out of any particular interest in fraud but for what the story tells us about the status of the manuscript at the end of the eighteenth century. If nothing else, the literary manuscript was a revered enough object to be worth forging. The public would pay to see it and to be in its presence.

I would like to consider the manuscript, the letter, and other objects of study that make up our research institutions' rich archival collections. I'm particularly interested in how our attitudes towards these objects have shifted over time, what has remained the same, and what opportunities may be posed by the fundamental change in the nature of the contemporary archive.

The Vogue of the Autograph

During the eighteenth and nineteenth centuries, when the vogue of autograph collecting was at its height, it was not uncommon for signatures to be clipped from letters and other documents to assemble in autograph albums. This popular fascination with the autograph corresponded with the explosion of print culture made possible by advances in printing processes. One can still find these relics, often in ornate Victorian bindings, in many of our special collections departments.

The Ransom Center paid silent homage to the practice when it installed windows with the signatures of authors represented in the Center's collections etched into the glass (at least in this instance no manuscripts were defaced in the process). It is quite common to come upon nineteenth century letters where the author's signature has been clipped from the bottom of the page and the mutilated letter left behind as being of secondary interest.

It was the signature, the personal mark of the author, which was the coveted object. The autograph was not so much an object of study as it was an object of veneration and devotion. On some level the expressive signature was a stand-in for the absent author in a way his or her words were not. While autograph collecting continues today, the signature often works in another way. Often it serves to differentiate the machine made object and fix that artifact (a best-selling author's trade book for example) in a particular place in time.

Manuscript editions emerged at the end of the nineteenth century and were conceived to differentiate the machine-made text in this way. Samuel Clemens, Walt Whitman, and Henry David Thoreau all had groups of manuscripts cannibalized for just this purpose. The Ransom Center's copy of the manuscript edition of Whitman's *Complete Works* includes an individual manuscript leaf of *Specimen Days* bound into the volume to create a unique work. In order to dispel any doubts about the authenticity of the text a notary public has affixed her seal certifying that "the accompanying sheet is a page of original manuscript." We have it on the authority of Miss. Annie B. Walters that the manuscript before us is from Whitman's hand.[2]

It was not until the twentieth century that newly conceived special collections departments began acquiring not manuscript leaves but entire archives. Within these bulky collections, however, the literary manuscript continued to hold its value as a coveted object of both wonder and study. What we are experiencing now, since the early 1990s, is a fundamental change in the form of the literary manuscript and, by extension, a fundamental change in the very nature of the archive itself.

The Computer-Generated Manuscript

While the dates may vary from one writer to another, those of us who work with collections of personal papers or archives can date the change quite precisely. For J. M. Coetzee it occurred between his 1983 novel *The Life and Times of Michael K* and his 1986 novel *Foe*. For Salman Rushdie it occurred relatively late, after the publication of *The Satanic Verses* in 1988 but before the publication of *The Moor's Last Sigh* in 1995. For Gabriel García Márquez it came early, after *Chronicle of a Death Foretold* in 1981 and before *Love in the Time of Cholera* in 1985. In between those two books he was awarded the Nobel Prize in Literature. He also began composing on a personal computer.

Holograph manuscript drafts long ago gave way to typescripts that have subsequently given way to the clean pointillism of the dot matrix printer with its own curiously vintage appearance.

It is safe to say virtually all textual production (what used to be called "writing") is done on a computer. "Every afternoon I pull my work out of the printer," García Márquez explained to an interviewer. "I take the pages to bed, I read them, and I make corrections and notes in the margin..... If they had given me a computer twenty years ago, I would have written twice as many books as I have."[3] These hand-corrected, computer-generated typescripts resemble the corrected typescripts of an

Part II: The Enduring Object

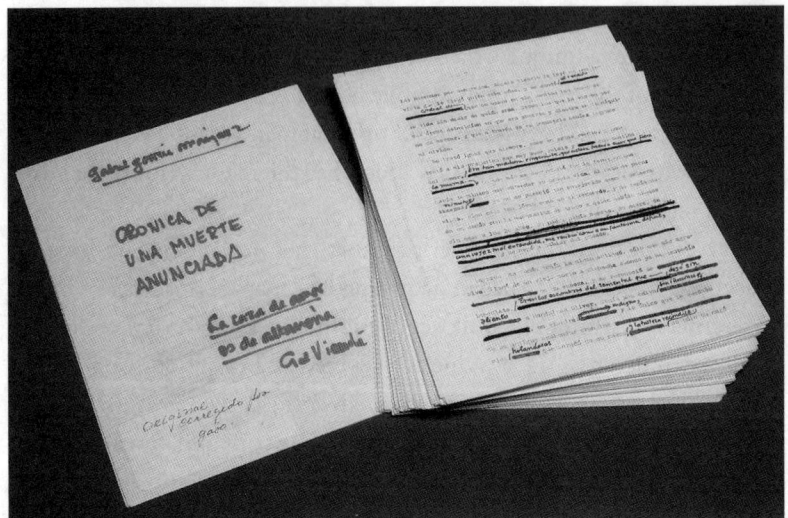

FIGURE 13.1. Corrected typescript of Gabriel García Márquez's *Crónica de una muerte anunciada* (*Chronicle of a Death Foretold*); Gabriel García Márquez papers, Harry Ransom Center, The University of Texas at Austin

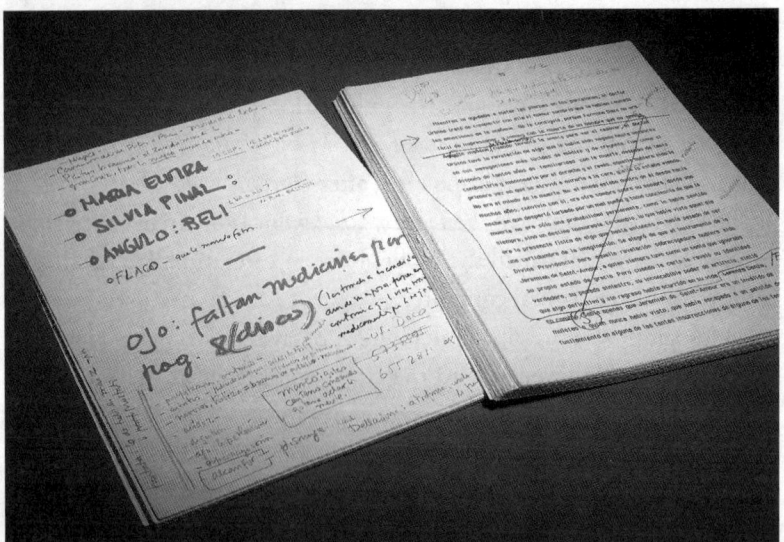

FIGURE 13.2. Computer-generated typescript of Gabriel García Márquez's *El amor en los tiempos del cólera* (*Love in the Time of Cholera*); Gabriel García Márquez papers, Harry Ransom Center, The University of Texas at Austin

Chapter 13: Objects of Study

FIGURE 13.3. Gabriel García Márquez at his Macintosh Plus

earlier time (see figures 13.1 and 13.2). The holograph emendation, like the autograph that differentiates the machine-made object, persists as a singular record of the work's composition.

But while García Márquez may have marked up his pages in bed, others complete their revisions at the computer keyboard itself, and it is not uncommon to find a literary manuscript exists only as a group of clean, unmarked pages of twenty-pound bond copy paper. The ease of on-screen revision, and the ease with which a new draft can be generated, means that an author may not labor over a typescript as he or she might have in an earlier time. It was simply too time-consuming to produce very many typescripts, while now computer-generated text can be produced with ease and at a great rate.

What this technological change means for the archive is that evidence of an author's creative choices may only become clear on close examination of textual differences among multiple copies. It is a painstaking form of study that frankly few in our reading rooms are engaged in.

Also entering our archives, often in great quantity, is all manner of digital storage media with no discernable evidence of the author's hand. The García Márquez archive at the Ransom Center includes the Macintosh Plus computer on which he wrote *Love in the Time of Cholera* (see figure 13.3), as well as an external hard drive, two PowerBooks, two Iomega zip disks, along with other digital storage media.

When floppies, 3½" diskettes, and other digital storage media began showing up in the contemporary writers' archives I was assembling at my university in the 1990s, our processing staff didn't quite know what to do with them. If we were lucky, the disks had been labeled in some fashion, and one could record that detail in a finding aid before placing it in a box. It wasn't practical to open the files to compare them with computer-generated typescripts elsewhere in the archive (nor would that have been a good idea, as digital archivists now tell us). In this regard, these born-digital files resemble the audiotape and other magnetic media that also resists easy archival appraisal.

Little wonder that some advised rendering the unfamiliar *familiar* by printing out the files and cataloging not the diskettes but these freshly minted "manuscripts" (a solution that reminds me of the British Library's practice for many years of binding loose manuscripts so they looked like a book). Further contributing to this blurring of distinction, some of our finding aids do not differentiate between a typescript produced on a typewriter and a computer-generated "typescript," though the former is a unique record of a creative work at one moment in its composition and the latter may exist in many multiples.

When the object is not a computer printout at all, but still a digital file, its ability to be reproduced is unlimited. The fragility of the storage medium itself in fact calls for replication and a schedule for refreshing that ephemeral digital data. Practice is still widely inconsistent, however, and a recent survey of British libraries and archives found that nearly half of the respondents simply do not accept digital storage media.[4]

What seems clear is that much is being lost, whether through a refusal to accept it, or through uncertainty over just what to do with it when it does come into our archives. Harvard recently discovered among the John Updike papers 5¼" program disks for Lotus Ami Pro word processing software, popular in the early 1990s, indicating there must at one time have been 5¼" floppies though none are present in the archive. Nor did any of his computers come with his archive.[5]

What did survive among the Updike papers, however, are forty-one 3½" diskettes dating from a later period of his writing life. It appears he used these to back up files and, on occasion, to mail stories and reviews back and forth to his editors at *The New Yorker* and elsewhere. While Updike was meticulous about saving drafts that he had printed out and revised, he did not show the same attitude toward the digital files themselves and discarded used disks and overwrote other files as he revised. In a bizarre twist, a literary scavenger rummaging through Updike's trash recovered some of these discarded diskettes, including one containing the author's files for his 1984 novel *The Witches of Eastwick*.[6]

Whether we welcome these developments or not, the form of the literary manuscript has forever changed. Boswell may not even recognize a contemporary manuscript, but *he would be able to read the words*. And that brings us to the crux of the matter. As long as these drafts reflect the creative decisions of the working writer, they will hold their research value as records of the creative process. They will persist as evidence of the writer's solitary struggle with his muse. I daresay future textual projects will adapt to these new manuscript forms, and, in time, we may even grow nostalgic for Apple's early fonts designed not for the beauty of their letter forms but for onscreen legibility.

Salman Rushdie

When I arrived at Salman Rushdie's London home to see his archive, I discovered he had stored his old and obsolete computers in a cupboard. Yes, I was told, these computers would be included with his "papers." Rushdie was represented in this sale by the literary agent Andrew Wylie, who was eager to emphasize the research potential of these machines.

"I foresee volumes of email correspondence that are frankly far more interesting than the traditional selection of written letters," Wylie noted. In asking us to shift our attention from the literary manuscript to Rushdie's email, Wylie was actually onto something important. He was commenting on the character of email—its conversational quality and its unguarded spontaneity—which is very different from the conventions of a formal letter. It is, he insisted, "a very, very valuable resource."[7]

Wylie more typically negotiates publishing contracts for his clients, and in this instance too he was intent on pushing the sale price for the Rushdie papers as high as he possibly could. In the end, however, no precedent was set for the value of the born-digital content in Rushdie's archive, since the purchase price did not differentiate what portion of the total was for the traditional paper-based archive and what portion, if any, for the born-digital archive. As long as an archive remains hybrid we will not have a clear precedent for the sale of its born-digital content. The Rushdie acquisition was negotiated without giving the digital files any specific value.

Why does this matter?

It may, in fact, matter a great deal. Whatever else we may have to say about the trade in writer's archives, it is that trade that has ensured the survival of countless collections of letters and manuscripts. It is that awareness of an archive's monetary value that has led to a high survival rate for scores of paper-based archives, and it therefore follows that uncertainty about the value of born-digital content may threaten the survival of our twenty-first century archives.

It has now been more than two decades since the widespread adoption of email in our homes and workplaces. Its penetration into all aspects of our daily lives suggests a digital archive of our electronic lives could easily run into tens or even hundreds of thousands of messages researchers at Stanford estimate.[8]

Ian McEwan

Since 1997 Ian McEwan has systematically archived his email correspondence. Unlike a paper-based archive where one may only find the incoming correspondence, the McEwan archive that the Ransom Center recently acquired contains both sides of the exchange. "I didn't set out to save all my emails," McEwan has explained. "I just didn't know how to get rid of them.... It's a mountain of 'see you at eight o'clock.' Every now and then there must be significant ones, but the sheer volume is very great."[9]

Yet it seems clear that the full range of life experience is documented in email communications, including some communications that in an earlier day might have been lost over a telephone line.

What's more, these email communications often lack the self-consciousness that characterizes a formal letter. The perceived ephemerality of the communication can lead to a high degree of candor. "I email a lot, so there's all sorts of stuff there," Rushdie said, "but don't ask me to remember what it is."[10]

The Archive of the Future

Our modern literary archives have been assembled to support particular types of critical inquiry. For many years the most privileged object within the archive has been the literary manuscript. These archives supported major textual projects of the 1950s and 1960s at a time when authorial intention seemed a realistic goal and one could still aspire to publish a "definitive edition" without embarrassment. Textual projects now seek less the stability of the text than its instability, leading to important digital editions that reconstruct not a singular and coherent authorial intention but the competing status of multiple texts at moments in time. The editors of the Mark Twain Project Online based at Berkeley note that "all texts...are permanently unstable," before offering the visitor to its website nine competing source texts for *The Adventures of Huckleberry Finn*.[11]

While the literary works entering our archives today may receive close textual analysis, we have decades to wait before they will become the basis of scholarly editions. Critical editions of Ian McEwan, Salman Rushdie, and John Updike are many years off, if indeed that textual interest emerges at all. What this means is we are capturing and preserving a highly ephemeral born-digital resource in hopes that these files will satisfy the curiosity of a distant and future reader.

Somewhere along the way, perhaps with the death of the author, the author became a corporate entity and archives become voluminous gatherings of all manner of materials documenting aspects of textual production. Cultural studies helped to expand the notion of textual objects and encouraged use of our archives to examine the historical interconnections of writers and communities of writers, the business of literary production, the processes of canonization, and reading practices among different communities of readers in different times and places.

The social aspect of these lines of inquiry will be illuminated by the large quantity of email making its way into our contemporary archives. For the near term it seems likely some of the heaviest research interest may well reside in the email communications of authors within their circle of friendships and associates. Interest in "the lives of the poets," to use Samuel Johnson's memorable phrase, seems likely to persist.

New Directions in Archival Scholarship

The born-digital archive may also come to support other forms of critical inquiry. When J. M. Coetzee was a graduate student at The University of Texas in the late 1960s, he wrote a dissertation inspired by a promising new form of textual study called "stylostatistics": the application of computer analysis to the linguistic features of texts.[12] Coetzee was following the linguist Bernard Bloch, who believed computer analysis could recognize recurring features of a text that even the most careful reader might never see. One of the by-products of large-scale digitization of books has been the opportunity for textual analysis, centered not on a single canonical author or work but on a corpus far larger than any one individual could ever hope to read.

At the Folger Shakespeare Library, researchers are conducting linguistic analysis on large collections of digitized text to learn more about word usage, metaphor, and genre in the sixteenth and seventeenth centuries. To pose just one question: Did Shakespeare really invent the many words he is said to have coined, or is his high scoring simply the result of his plays serving as preferred source texts for lexicographers of an earlier day? What would the linguistic analysis of a large corpus of seventeenth-century texts tell us about Shakespeare's inventiveness; about distinctive features of comedy, history, and tragedy; about other genres, including nonfiction prose? How would those answers differ if the source texts were not a small number of "literary" texts but a vast corpus of many thousands of literary and nonliterary texts.[13] For the first time, researchers have the tools to answer such questions.

The explosion of born-digital content in our contemporary archives may offer us the ability to perform similar analysis on large bodies of electronic texts accumulating in our special collections. As the quantity of this born-digital content grows, it seems likely that the next decade will see the further development of tools for the analysis and manipulation of large bodies of electronic communications. The scale alone will require it.

Researchers at Stanford are already experimenting with tools that infer social groups within a vast body of tens of thousands of email messages based on a grouping algorithm. Further "sentiment analysis," based on textual cues, can be mapped using visualization techniques. While we may recoil from machine-based analysis, which seems a poor substitute for reading, the further development of these kinds of tools will only become more necessary as the quantity of digital content grows too large to be easily read.

Greater facility with digital content within our archives will, I predict, bring renewed attention to long-neglected elements of the archive, those requiring digital reformatting, such as sound and moving image recordings. It seems likely this interest will only accelerate with the increasing acceptance of new forms of digital publication. The monograph is no longer the only product our researchers may hope to produce. They may be creating a website, a database, or some form of visualization that incorporates image and sound.

The web offers us a platform for innovative forms of publication like that my Texas colleague has undertaken on the website *What Jane Saw*.[14] This web-based publication provides a visual simulation of the British Institution gallery in Pall Mall, which we know from her diaries Jane Austen visited on May 24, 1813. Visitors to the site can move into a three-dimensional space and view high-quality digital images of the Joshua Reynolds paintings that Jane Austen viewed on that day. This online gallery space serves as a superstructure on which a rich layer of historical and contextual information is provided about Austen, Reynolds, and the nineteenth-century museum experience.

While copyright will continue to hinder the full exploitation of literary texts for years to come, the open access movement and the development of nonrestrictive licensing policies is encouraging other nontraditional uses of our archives. All evidence suggests that the transformation that is under way in our archives will enable entirely new sets of questions not necessarily based on reading. Questions like "How distinctive was Shakespeare's speech?" and "What did Jane Austen see?"

What these developments also highlight for us, I trust, are fundamental changes in the object of study itself. While some researchers will continue to visit the born-digital archive to "read" a work and to compare one manifestation of a text with earlier and later versions, others will be looking for entirely new forms of evidence of the creative process.

Within the community examining these questions are some who wish to deploy the techniques of law enforcement and apply tools for digital forensics to digital archives by recovering keystrokes and deleted files, the equivalent of reading through a struck-through passage of a manuscript. Others are committed to emulating the desktop environment of the author's computer: what Salman Rushdie saw each morning when he powered up his personal computer, which versions of software he used, his file structure, and his naming conventions. For others the growing body of electronic content is a source of data ripe for machine analysis of the kind researchers at Stanford are undertaking.

Ironically, the great promise of digital technology, built as it is on a network of interconnected computers, is constrained by the privacy and copyright concerns of living figures. Salman Rushdie may have been able to use the Internet to participate in a global literary community linking London, New York, and Mumbai, but his born-digital archive enjoys none of those benefits. One must fly to Atlanta and drive to Emory University to read the email communications that he once transmitted from London to New York with a keystroke. Files that were once transmitted instantly across great distances are now bound to a reading room desk like some medieval scriptorium.

The ability to perform analysis on a lifetime's body of electronic communications, or other large bodies of digital content, will lead to increasingly urgent questions about the privacy rights of individuals in a culture already deeply conflicted about the boundaries of public and private. We are increasingly capturing born-digital content as a regular processing activity, and the protocols for stabilizing that content and ensuring its integrity over time are emerging. What is most needed now are not tools but policies that will guide the access and use of this rich resource.

Technological change is creating new objects of study within our archives, and it follows that surprising new questions will be asked of this resource. Even amid these changes, however, the archive remains, in some persistent ways, remarkably constant. It is important that we remember an archive is more than a site of questioning and interrogation. Much of the power of the objects we hold in fact derives not from their informational content but from their persistent presence over time.

When the novelist Zadie Smith was asked what would likely become of her digital archive, she replied, "I guess it will go the way of everything else I write on the computer—oblivion."[15] Resistance to oblivion has always been one of our libraries' most meaningful roles. Manuscripts, letters, even a clipped autograph fill an absence and are evidence of a provisional victory over time. On some level the question for us is whether that absence can be filled by something as insubstantial, and infinitely replicable, as an electrical current moving over a silicon chip. To those seeking an answer to that question, I would simply suggest the ephemeral nature of our special collections has always been a surprising source of their power.

NOTES

1. S. Schoenbaum, *Shakespeare's Lives* (Oxford: Clarendon Press, 1991), 150.
2. Walt Whitman, *Complete Works of Walt Whitman*, Author's Manuscript Edition (New York: Putnam's Sons, 1902).
3. Raymond Leslie Williams, "The Visual Arts, the Poetization of Space and Writing: An Interview with Gabriel García Márquez," *PMLA* 104, no. 4 (March 1989): 131–40.
4. "Report on a Survey of GLAM Members' Acquisitions Policy and Practice," GLAM: Group for Literary Archives and Manuscripts, http://glam-archives.org.uk/wp-content/uploads/2011/02/survrep.pdf.
5. Matthew Kirschenbaum, "Operating Systems of the Mind: Bibliography after Word Processing (The Example of Updike)," *Papers of the Bibliographical Society of America* 108, no. 4 (2014): 381–412.
6. Adrienne LaFrance, "The Man Who Made Off with John Updike's Trash," *The Atlantic* (August 28, 2014), www.theatlantic.com/entertainment/archive/2014/08/the-man-who-made-off-with-john-updikes-trash/379213/.
7. Rachel Donadio, "Literary Letters, Lost in Cyberspace," *New York Times Book Review* (Sept. 4, 2006): 15.
8. Sudheendra Hangal, Monica Lam, and Jeffrey Heer, "Muse: Reviving Memories Using Email Archives," *Proceedings of the 24th Annual ASTM Symposium on User Interface Software and Technology* (New York: Association for Computing Machinery, 2011).
9. "A Literary Lion's Latest Obsession," Brenda Cronin, *The Wall Street Journal* (Sept. 5, 2014): D7.
10. Donadio, 15.
11. "'Textual Editing at the Mark Twain' Project: A Brief Account," Mark Twain Papers and Project, www.marktwainproject.org/about_hirst_essay.shtml.

12. J. M. Coetzee, "English Fiction of Samuel Beckett: An Essay in Stylistic Analysis" (PhD dissertation, The University of Texas at Austin, 1969), 6.
13. Michael Witmore, "Data-Mining Shakespeare," Director's Lecture Series, Folger Shakespeare Library, October 26, 2011.
14. Janine Barcus, Department of English, The University of Texas at Austin, what janesaw.org.
15. Donadio, 15.

PART III

From Periphery

to Center

Enabling access to unique collections in a variety of ways is becoming the core work of research libraries.

PART III

From Periphery to Center

CHAPTER 14

Considering the Present

Special Collections Are the Meal, Not the Dessert

JAY SATTERFIELD

Sometimes when I am getting a particularly delicate special collections item for someone, I set it up in a cradle at his or her table—then, often with a little flourish, I joke, "Hi, my name is Jay, and I'll be your server today. I hope you enjoy your book!" It is a nice way to break the intimidating formality that may have crept into the situation. It fits perfectly with the concept of special collections as a meal rather than a dessert, but also with our most basic philosophy in Rauner Special Collections Library at Dartmouth College. We want using special collections to be a mundane act—like going to the local college restaurant and getting some lunch. We want students to see that an item is located in special collections and think "no big deal," and head over to use it. There should not be any hassles involved. At the same time, we want them to absolutely love the experience. So much so, that when they step out of the door, they have to stop on the steps of the building and call their parents because they cannot believe what they were just able to do. We want mundane boredom punctuated with an exquisite and transcendent moment. Think of it as a really good meal at a casual diner.

We are certainly not there yet. Lots of people are still nervous about using special collections, but we have made structural changes to reduce that fear. Ten years ago we made a conscious decision to remake ourselves. We had great collections, especially for an institution of our size. Dartmouth has been around a long time, and for about half of its history, it has been a relatively wealthy institution, and it has a long tradition of nurturing a devoted alumni base eager to give back. As a result of over two centuries of devoted alumni building up impressive private collections and then donating them to Dartmouth, then later establishing endowments for acquisitions, we have collections that can really work for us. We have a beautiful facility. But, other than serving a few devoted faculty, some visiting researchers, and some adventurous students, the collections were coming nowhere near to achieving their potential.

I had somewhat narrowly conceived of special collections as a center for the curriculum. The college archivist, Peter Carini, quickly humbled me by aiming higher and being far more eloquent in stating, "No, we should become the center for the intellectual life of the College." That resonated with our staff. They had been hungering to share their deep knowledge and appreciation for the collections. They saw an opportunity to blow open the doors to the building, which has some qualities of a mausoleum from the outside, and turn the campus on to the amazingly cool materials held within. Without that immediate and full embrace by our staff, I am not sure what we would have been able to achieve. But with it, we went from hosting five or six classes a year in a sleepy reading room to the point where three years ago we had to add a third classroom to accommodate demand. In 2013–14, 115 different classes accounting for 265 sessions used the collections directly. These classes came from 25 different departments and brought in over 1,600 students on a campus with only 4,200 students. Over a third of the student body came in that year—and that was just for classes. We are nearing a saturation of the curriculum and approaching a goal we once thought of as a purely aspirational pipe dream: that by the time they graduate from Dartmouth, every student will have had a meaningful encounter with our materials. By meaningful, we mean in their hands, in close interrogation, and learning from the objects. Last month, we even worked with a computer science class on Computational Fabrication (3D printing), using books that do something interesting with three-dimensional space within the confines of the printed page, or in the case of *Your House* by Olafur Eliasson, the laser cut page. Over the course of their four years of college, we are getting close to catching all of the students.

Our first step was a risky one. We are a not a small place—we have an FTE of thirteen—but neither are we one of the colossal players in the special collections world. The curatorial model, with one curator responsible for the archives, another for rare books, and a third for manuscripts, did not seem suited to an institution of our size with collections of our scope, nor did it fit with our vision of fully integrating the collections. Dartmouth as an institution always straddles this line between the aspirations, resources, and faculty of a major research university and the ideal of a small liberal arts college devoted to excellence in undergraduate education. We feel the same pressure in special collections and needed a structure to align ourselves better with the larger institution. So we dumped the curatorial model and moved to a functional model. One person as head of the department with major administrative functions, another in charge of all of the processing activities, and a third focused on reader services. All three devote considerable time and energy to outreach and education by pushing the collections into the intellectual life of the College. I am not the curator of anything, nor are any of my cohorts in special collections. Three of us are empowered to make collection development decisions, but we take advice broadly. We have a loose division of duties in collection development based on our expertise, but the lines are permeable, and create ample opportunities to discuss potential acquisitions from multiple viewpoints. The routing slips on our dealer catalogs are long and include any member of the staff who wants to see them. Recently we bought a manuscript diary based on our intern's recommendation. As a recent graduate of Dartmouth she may not have known the collections well, but she was closer to the students than the rest of us. Her instinct was right on target: the diary was used by a student in the reading room shortly after we acquired it. It was a perfect fit for an assignment—it was a brilliant acquisition, which the rest of us had overlooked because we did not notice a hook into curriculum or into current students' interests. While most of our collection development decisions are made by a few people, many contribute.

We felt the curatorial model was limiting librarians' roles, siloing collections, discouraging the creative use of materials across collections, and hampering access. Many curators fall into the trap of thinking in the first person singular possessive and their position descriptions and rewards structures encourage this. They talk of "my" collections and "my" faculty. At Rauner Library "we" have collections and "we" have users. Since we made the shift to the functional model, user satisfaction and overall use of the collections has risen, and class use has exploded. In parallel good news, our processing backlog has shrunk to a fraction of what it was, and we are no longer adding to the backlog. We never face the problem of a rare book curator holding a manuscript in her hand with a puzzled look, or a modern manuscript curator ignoring a pile of books in his office that arrived with a new manuscript collection, because neither had the energy to cross boundaries to get them processed. We think it was the right move—the functional model freed us and opened the collections.

A good example of the benefits we gained by dropping curatorial territoriality is a class session that employs materials from the college archives, the rare book collections, and the manuscript collections to build out a historical narrative. It is very much an active learning exercise where the students have ownership of the materials and the story that emerges from them.

For a class of sixteen students, we select eight items on a common theme. We do not explain how the documents are related; we simply give them to the students—one item for every two people. We ask each pair of students to do three seemingly simple things. First, they need to identify the item (what is it: a letter, a picture, a book?). Second, they need to tell the class the object's information value—in other words, what is it telling them? And third, and this is crucial, they need to explain what questions the document leads them to ask. What do they want to know more about after reading it?

The first item is a January 1777 petition to the Town of Hanover, New Hampshire, from a group of students asking for permission to inoculate themselves from smallpox, which had recently entered the area. The document also has a response from the town select board granting the permission as long as the students isolate themselves in a house just over the town line in a rural area of Lebanon, New Hampshire. The next group gets a prescription from a Dr. Tiffany, dated January 1777, for a mixture to be taken two weeks prior to inoculation. The prescription results in a fairly strong purging of the system. The third group receives a letter signed by Ebenezer Hasletine, dated February 12, 1777, to his brother explaining that he was recently inoculated for smallpox. It relays that a group of the "scholars" were inoculated and came through fine, but a Native American girl caught it "the natural way."

Then we switch to published sources. The fourth group gets William Douglass's *A Summary, Historical and Political, of the First Planting, Progressive Improvements, and Present State of the British Settlements in North America* (Boston: D. Fowle, 1753). We bookmarked "A Digression concerning the Small-Pox" that presents statistical information on the prevalence of the disease in the colonies. The fifth group looks at *Acts and Laws of the State of New Hampshire* (Exeter: Z. Fowle, 1780). It is the first published law book of the new State of New Hampshire. In it, the students see the first laws passed by the state after the Declaration of Independence, including one passed in December 1776 designed to prevent the spread of smallpox. It states that no one may be inoculated without first getting the permission of the town's select board. Failure to do so will result in a fine of thirty-five pounds. The sixth item is *The Life of the Late Reverend, Learned and Pious Mr. Jonathan Edwards* (Boston: S. Kneeland, 1765). The passage marked explains that Edwards became the president of what would become Princeton University and was inoculated for smallpox as a preventative. Complications set in and he died. The seventh and eighth groups receive two older pieces from 1722 that are part of a pamphlet war debating the effectiveness and morality of inoculation. Benjamin Coleman's *Narrative of the Method and Success of Inoculating the Small Pox in New England* (London: Emanuel Matthews, 1722) and Legard Sparham's *Reasons against the Practice of Inoculating the Small-Pox* (London: Benj. and Sam. Tooke, 1722).

What happens is pretty amazing. We give the students about fifteen minutes to work with the documents in pairs, then we go around the room and each pair reports out to the class. First, what is it? Second, what does it tell them? And third, what questions do they have? Ideally—and it almost always works—the questions from one pair are answered by the documents in the hands of other pairs. The documents form a web of context and meaning that contribute to a narrative that relates to smallpox and Dartmouth's past. After everyone has presented, during which lots of connections become apparent, and at least a few students begin wiggling with excitement, we ask for one volunteer to "tell the story." We have done this dozens of times with different suites of material (we call them "teachable packages"), and never had any trouble getting a volunteer—we usually have several. We pick one person, and he or she pieces together a disjointed, moderately accurate story that ties the documents together. In this case, that a smallpox epidemic hit the Hanover area in 1777 and several Dartmouth students decided to take the inoculation. They were isolated, inoculated, and emerged healthy, although one local from the town got sick and risked spreading the illness more broadly in the community. Also that, for some reason, inoculation was dangerous, controversial, and regulated by law.

They miss some things, and make some outlandish assumptions. They often confuse inoculation, which is the introduction of the live smallpox pathogen into a scratch, with vaccination, which is far safer. A few sources, like the *History of the Colonies,* or the *Life of Edwards,* might get left out altogether in the first pass. The story is incomplete and has at least a few serious errors in it. That is when we get to work. After congratulating the brave student for doing such a good job, we ask the class to build on the narrative, correct it, and improve it. After hearing one student relate the story, others see new bits of information in their documents that contribute to the narrative. They are able to make new connections and add to the story. It is usually at this point that someone figures out the letter about the inoculation was signed by one of original petitioners and people start putting together dates, and the less obviously connected sources come into play. By the end of the class we have usually done a pretty good job of getting an accurate story told, acknowledging what we do not know, and where we made assumptions that need to be verified from other sources. We also talk about the value of secondary sources used alongside these primary sources.

The session works for a couple of reasons. First, there is no curator interpreting the story. Nobody in the room is playing the role of an expert that the students can question and rely on. They are responsible for the narrative and they own it. Second, since we often use exercises like this in freshman writing classes, we know that students are excited about their new home at Dartmouth and hungry for information about its past. They are literally within a few hundred yards of where many of these documents were produced over two centuries ago, and they are deeply intrigued with the history of the place. The aura of the original is another motivator—they have the real thing in hand, and they value its information more than if it were a photocopy or a digital surrogate. But, most importantly, they are in an arena of communal discovery. They might be working in pairs, but they are building the story as a group because each pair is only contributing a fragment. The session really has nothing to do with smallpox or Dartmouth history. It is about the students learning how primary sources work: how they can tell you so much in context, and so little in isolation. How they can bring clarity and bring confusion, and how they are dependent on each other for meaning. The thrill of discovery and interconnectivity is present in all that the students are doing.

The lesson for special collections is that history is not written from just rare books, just institutional records, or just manuscript collections. The integration of these sources is *essential* for building meaning. Students and scholars should not see them in isolation, and we should strive to avoid institutional structures that create that isolation. We all know this, but we also all know individual curators who undermine this holistic approach to our collections. In a very real way, having dropped the curatorial model allowed us the freedom to assemble this class. It also drove me all through the department, talking with different staff members, asking, "I need a document that tells me this—do you know where to find one?" Just as the students created meaning out of the documents by working together, we built the session collaboratively across what some would consider curatorial boundaries. Interestingly, the last item used in the session, the pamphlet arguing against inoculation, was not in the collections the first time we taught this class. We saw it in a dealer catalog a few months later and snapped it up for the connections it would make and knowing how well it would interact with the College Archives. We are constantly on the lookout for stories in the collection that can be spun out like the smallpox exercise, and we shop for an item or two that will transform them into "teachable packages." Our collection development is shaped by these needs that cross curatorial boundaries.

A parallel to subjugating curatorial control is played out in the relinquishing of control of the classroom experience to the students. Morgan Swan, our special collections education and outreach librarian, calls the process of the class just described as "exuberant chaos," and he is a big advocate for embracing it. It is a concept that freaks out a lot of special collections librarians. Most are into the exuberant side of things. We are all junkies for that moment of turning someone on to something really amazing in our collections. There is a kind of contact high watching someone see Hooke's *Micrographia* for the first time, or handle a 600-year-old manuscript, or read a cranky letter from Ezra Pound to Robert Frost. We start to get jaded in our daily interactions with our books and documents, but the rush of an undergraduate on rare materials jolts us back in time and space, just like it carries them into a new place.

But chaos? Well, that is not usually associated with the rarified air of special collections. It should be. Chaos is a space where people overcome inhibitions and open themselves to new experiences and learning. Think of it as a moment of anti-structure in your overly structured day, where things are turned on their heads, where the students run the class, and the conversation is based on what they are experiencing. The librarian's role is to pluck out the moments of clarity and reiterate them, add bits and pieces of context to allow the students' observations to mature into something beyond an initial impression, and let the experiential moment define the class.

It is harder than what a lot of us are used to. When we *present* materials we have control. We dictate the pace, highlight the parts of each object that we want the students to see, make sure we come to some conclusions that we feel are important, and do not need to worry about ideas flying out of left field that disrupt our end goals. With the exuberant chaos (which really is just another way of saying active learning, but expressed in a more lively way), our control is gone. We do not *really* know where the class will go, and we have to be on our toes every second to follow along and grab what we can. That is hard for a lot of people. We know why a certain object is super cool, and we could talk for hours about the awesomeness of something like the *Nuremberg Chronicle,* or a little pamphlet from the Zoot Suit riots, or Lewis Carroll's Alice portrayed as a 1920s flapper. But we have to subjugate that impulse and let the students find a fragment of that awesomeness and make it their own. That's hard, watching them miss something about a book or a manuscript that we think is amazing. That is chaotic, but that is learning. Old school "show and tell" is really fun for the students, and allows us to share our deep knowledge of the collections, but I doubt much actual learning occurs.

Selection of materials becomes crucial. There is a lot of upfront work involved in assembling something like the smallpox exercise, and this is where we are curators of another sort: assembling materials from across collections to tell a story, not unlike doing an exhibit without item labels or text. There are so many documents, but which eight do the job? None of them should tell too much, but each should contribute in its own unique way. The teaching, the control we are used to, takes place well before the session, when we load the dice with a selection of material that takes students in the right direction and facilitates their discoveries. In a sense, the *teaching* is done *outside* of the classroom—*inside* of the classroom is where *learning* happens.

This plays out in the digital world as well. Dartmouth is fortunate to have a fabulous polar research collection, the Stefansson collection. There is a large class taught each year in Environmental Studies on the earth's polar regions. The culminating research project has each student write a paper on a contemporary issue related to the Arctic or Antarctic that they must set into a historical context. The faculty member requires that at least two of the sources come from the Stefansson collection. There are usually around seventy students in the class, and we get mobbed every May. A few years ago, with the help of a grant from the Delmas Foundation, we digitized the *Encyclopedia Arctica*. It is a 15,000-page draft of an encyclopedia commissioned by the US Navy and edited by Vilhjalmur Stefansson. It was almost completed in 1951 when the Navy pulled the plug on the project because of Stefansson's loose ties to the Communist Party. Ironically, the Navy wanted the encyclopedia created because of the growing importance of the Arctic during the Cold War, but it was Cold War paranoia that killed the project. It is a terrific window into what exactly was known about the Arctic regions in 1951. Much to the students' delight, the unpublished encyclopedia can count as one of their sources.

Since we digitized the *Encyclopedia Arctica* and made it keyword searchable, the students have produced better papers and gone into more depth. They used to come to us with an idea, but with little notion of how to set it into historical context. We always had a session with the class devoted to the physical objects, where we showed materials from the collection—printed books, ephemera, and manuscripts—to give them ideas about how to make sense of the materials, but with a class that large, it was difficult to do anything interactive like the smallpox exercise. Now they use the *Encyclopedia Arctica* at all hours of the day and night to investigate their topics. By the time they come to special collections, they have context and narrowly defined researchable questions that we can help them explore more fully in the Stefansson collection. The faculty member who teaches the class commented that after we made the *Encyclopedia Arctica* keyword searchable, the papers improved dramatically and the overall depth of research surpassed his expectations. I think it helps that we are not mediating the experience with the *Encyclopedia Arctica*. The students are stumbling through a somewhat confusing source while having a personal moment of perhaps not-so-exuberant chaos. But from that struggle, they are finding the questions they really want to research.

There are some parallels in our philosophy of letting go in the classroom that resonate with other work we do. Michelle Light has made a very persuasive case for letting go of any rights enforcement we do—stop requiring people to ask permission to use images from our collections and stop charging use fees.[1] We have to continually push back on copyright holders who want collections locked down. As we digitize our collections, we should open them as widely as possible and create the structures for creative, easy, and free use and reuse of the materials. Dartmouth puts most of its collections into ContentDM—it holds materials and allows them to be downloaded, but it puts them into a narrow silo that is not easily indexed by search engines. If you search for a collection that is digitized, you will find it, but for the most part, we have hidden the individual items from search engines and inadvertently hidden them from most of the world.

When we first put up a digital collection, we wanted to provide layers of context so people would read the documents the "correct" way. The digital was just another realm for us to "show" our collections. We should let go of that notion. People will make of the materials what they will. Through creative reuse of digitized collections, they will build multiple contexts around the materials that will bring new meaning. As a profession, we were pretty much always comfortable with that in our reading room, with lone scholars, but it made a lot of us nervous in the digital world. We can see where that confusion can take people in a classroom, and so should allow it to happen in other venues as well. It is a good confusion: chaotic, exuberant, and productive. New truths emerge alongside a lot of dead ends, but it is worth it. That is all part of giving up the gatekeeper role our profession has played for too long—we give that up in our reading rooms, but now we need to continue that online and in our classrooms.

We are still being gatekeepers no matter how hard we try to escape it. But it is not so much whom we let use the materials or how we let them use them, but what materials we have in the first place. The gatekeeping function is in selection, what we allow into the collections in the first place. And we have to be so selective. We must pass by so much more than we can possibly save. For most of the second half of the twentieth century, special collections went wild collecting. New historical methods and interests made us look at our collections and curse ourselves—we felt we had been collecting all the wrong things. Our collections were built to support scholarship that was becoming less relevant, and we saw gaping holes everywhere. So we responded by trying to collect everything. And that resulted in hundred-year processing backlogs for a lot of us. Now, even with a processing philosophy that allows us to provide adequate access much more quickly, we still cannot collect everything.

It does not always work the way we want it to. The Computational Computing class shows some of the good and bad from exuberant chaos. We did this class using a speed-dating technique that works well when we want to give students a lot of exposure, but not necessarily much depth. Basically, students spend a little time getting to know many books in short, concentrated bursts of interaction. We only used six books. The first book, Eliasson's *Your House* (New York: Library Council of the Museum of Modern Art, 2006), we looked at as a group. We turned the pages and the students made comments as we went. Then the other five books—all of which played on three-dimensional space—were laid out on tables and the students moved around the room in groups that spent about eight minutes with each book.

As the students worked directly with the materials, the faculty member and I milled around. We usually do this to steer them if they are going awry, or add a little context if they look too baffled. But we did not really need to do anything. The students were very busy interacting with the books—playing with them and having what *appeared* to be revelatory moments. With ten minutes left in the class, we stopped and asked the students what they saw that they could apply to their projects. After fifty-five minutes of raucous excitement, we faced a room of total silence. I am very patient in those situations. I'll wait it out by counting to thirty slowly in my head. Someone always speaks before I get there. When I got into the mid-twenties, when I was beginning to squirm as much as the students were, one of them offered up, "I liked the way the books represented interior space." Well, it was a start, but not really what we were looking for. Things did not get much better after that and we had a halting, fairly shallow discussion. Something about the structure of the session, the materials we selected, or the expectations the students brought with them, made them unable to make the turn to the practical. They loved the stuff, but they were not able to do anything other than marvel at it. They might just have needed more time to process what they saw. But, at the moment, it felt like it had been a waste of time. The faculty member and I *so* wanted to *tell* them how it applied—answer our own questions. But we did not. That only would have made us feel better without enhancing their learning.

Dartmouth is full of high-achieving students. The school does a very good job of attracting adventurous thinkers: students who are game to try out new ideas. But they are also terrified of failure. These have always been top students and the fear of offering up something that is wrong can silence them and stifle the effectiveness of the chaotic approach. Failure is part of the process of learning and we need to be clear that failure is acceptable in the classroom. We may have just positioned the conversation poorly, so the students were afraid of being wrong and that kept them silent. Perhaps if we had not looked at one book carefully at the start, they would have felt more free to experiment with their ideas. The class was not a success, even though it was lots of fun.

The exuberant chaos of the classroom is how we approach so much of our work. Let the interactions occur and see where they go. Collect those things we think will be useful. Sometimes they flop, but most of the time they work. But the important thing is that we position our collections so that they can serve people in the best way. For Dartmouth this meant shifting our structure as a department and realigning our focus. Returning to our original metaphor of special collections as the meal, there is a diner called Lou's in Hanover that is popular with the students. It opened right after World War II and has fed generations of students. There is nothing fancy about it, the beef is not grass-fed, and I do not think there is anything consciously organic on the menu, but the food is all made from scratch, and it has an authenticity that is really appealing. The place does not have any pretentions, and people do not feel "special" going there, but they always get a good meal. That should be our philosophy with our collections. Stop treating them like fine dining and think of them as basic nutrition for the scholarly world and for our students. The work we do with classes is not a bit of extra credit or a treat to celebrate the end of the term. It should be the meat of the course—interactions with materials to make the abstract concrete and further the goals of the class. As an added bonus, for most students it is the sweetest moment in the day.

NOTE

1. Michelle Light, "Controlling Goods or Promoting the Public Good: Choices for Special Collections in the Marketplace," *RBM* (Spring 2015): 48–63.

CHAPTER 15

Teaching with Special Collections

CHRISTOPH IRMSCHER

"Christmas... is a cheating holiday," wrote Bartolomeo Vanzetti, on December 28, 1926, to Mary Donovan, the secretary of the Sacco and Vanzetti Defense Committee and one of his regular visitors in Charlestown State Prison. She had sent him a Christmas card. Vanzetti's problem with everyone's favorite holiday was this: once a year, right in time for those supposedly special couple of days, people would pretend to be good—an attitude that, when it was not merely a "bad illusion," was simply "rank hypocracy."[1] The word is vintage Vanzetti: recognizable enough to make sense but, at the same time, entirely original and weird, evoking new meanings the conventional spelling won't gesture at. I like the term "hypocracy" applied to the democratic and, in Vanzetti's view, pseudo-Christian United States, whose courts had falsely kept imprisoned a poor Italian fishmonger for a murder many still believe he couldn't have committed. Vanzetti found support in a quip by Mark Twain he remembered, namely that the only useful holiday we celebrate is April Fools' Day, since it reminds us of what we really are during the rest of the year.[2] "Holy macherel," Vanzetti exclaims at the end of this brief reflection, and then interrupts himself, since he's actually not sure about how to spell "mackerel." "Holy" is not a problem, but the name of the fish is, even though fish used to be Vanzetti's business. He tries out an alternative spelling ("makerel"), but then throws in the towel. "I am only sure of holy, though fish peddler," he quipped. How ironic that, at the end of this train of thought, religion seems to be the place where Vanzetti is on firm ground.

131

Vanzetti's anti-Christmas diatribe is a rich document. Written on a bifold of cheap, lined paper, in Vanzetti's careful, slanting handwriting, neat as a schoolboy's, it gives us a sense of the depth of the man's mind. The letter was published in 1928, in Gardner Jackson and Marion Frankfurter's edition of the Sacco and Vanzetti letters, the standard text quoted by everybody and still available as a Penguin paperback today. But when one checks her version of Vanzetti's missive, one finds that the editors have simply (and without noting so) corrected his wayward spelling, thus removing, as a student of mine, Megan Jones, put it, "any humor from the joke."[3]

Vanzetti's autograph letter, along with fifty-seven others by him, is part of the Hapgood Mss. at the Lilly Library at Indiana University Bloomington.[4] Megan read Vanzetti as an assignment for a class I taught a few years ago, English L-460, Modern Manuscripts. When Megan compared the handwritten version of his Christmas letter with the one that was printed in the Jackson and Frankfurter edition, she was at first surprised at the discrepancies. Then she became annoyed. Bartolomeo Vanzetti was executed seven months after his Christmas reflection, after two trials in which exonerating evidence—including an actual confession by a career criminal—was ignored or diminished, and the judge was heard bragging outside of court about what he had done to those "anarchistic bastards." "Rank hypocracy," in Vanzetti's own words. Or, as a red armband distributed by the Sacco-Vanzetti Committee (which can also be found in the Lilly's collection) stated: "Justice Crucified."[5] The fact that the executed Boston fishmonger's voice had been corrupted by his editors—well-meaning though they were—seemed to her as if insult had been added to injury. Megan began to spend more and more time in the Lilly's Reading Room until she had transcribed most of Vanzetti's letters. What had begun as a class assignment grew into Megan's sixty-three-page Honors thesis submitted in 2014, "Vanzetti's Voice: A Critical Look at the Letters of Bartolomeo Vanzetti."

■ ■ ■

The idea behind English L-460 was a simple one. And yet I don't think a similar concept had been used for a class before, at least not by one of my colleagues at Indiana University Bloomington. The librarians at the Lilly Library do teach individual sessions for classes at the request of faculty members, and they regularly develop classes for graduate students in Indiana University's library science program. My course, however, was intended for English majors, not library science students. For several years, I had become more and more dissatisfied with the way we teach our undergraduates in the humanities. While even freshmen in the natural sciences gain practical experience, for example, by working in a professor's lab, most of our regular courses are either lecture- or discussion-based, divorced from any professional context in which our students might find themselves after they graduate. Defenders of the traditional role of the humanities see this as an asset rather than a liability, and with good reason. And yet, the more committed of my students had for years been asking me about the work that I do outside the classroom. Like many of my colleagues, I had kept my identity as a scholar separate from my role as a teacher, resigning myself to advocacy for the more general relevance of my subject to a student's academic education, always mindful of the miniscule percentage of English majors that go on to pursue a graduate degree in the discipline I had chosen. But I had not been happy doing so: I found myself longing for a different way of interacting with my students, one that would connect what I taught to some of the reasons why I had devoted my life as a researcher and writer to working with texts. I am an archival scholar and editor as well as a biographer of Henry Wadsworth Longfellow, Louis Agassiz, and, more recently, Max Eastman. The book-club model of the typical English class, in which we celebrate the privileged space opened up by the literary text as a source of superior insight, had never fully worked for me. Some of the subjects of my research—Louis Agassiz was a scientist and Max Eastman mostly a political writer and pundit—did not fit any narrow "literary" categories anyway. To make matters worse, I am at best a reluctant convert to literary theory, the classic English Department compensation for the alleged lack of professional or "scientific" rigor in our discipline.[6]

    What I realized I wanted to create was a course that would allow my students to get a glimpse of the kind of work I do as a scholar, a course that would enable them to think of themselves not just a learners but, potentially and for the space of one semester, as my colleagues. L-460, as I imagined it, would help me to break down that wall between teaching and research. At the heart of the class I was envisioning was the close encounter with the artifact itself. For me, at the beginning of my love affair with libraries, was the way they smelled, the way books or old letters felt when I picked them up, the sound the pages made when I turned them. In my class, I would encourage my students to read, see, touch, and smell whatever they had decided to find out more about. (The Lilly, which prides itself on providing direct access to their materials, is a fantastic place in which to make such encounters happen). If this approach reminds you of the anecdote of the fish Louis Agassiz had asked his students to draw until it started reeking so badly that they couldn't carry on—Ezra Pound famously used it in his *ABC of Reading*—that is not entirely inappropriate.[7] Except that books and manuscripts don't decompose, at least not that fast. I realized then, as I still do, that my method, superficially at least, appears to buck the trend towards digitization in recent thinking about the future of special collections. But in fact, I knew that I would actively encourage my students to produce digital versions of their materials, would ask them to use their cellphones and cameras to take pictures or get the Lilly's photographer to produce professional scans for us. And I would require them to present the results of their work in electronic, publicly shareable form on websites and as web exhibits. To be sure, my model depends on students crossing the physical threshold of the library, a place many of them had never visited. But my ultimate goal was to "demystify" special collections, to establish them as a place not unlike but in fact very much like the rest of the campus or, for that matter, the world. A place that was not apart from, but a part of their community.[8]

When I taught the class, student engagement surpassed my expectations. So far I have offered English L-460 just once, but I have incorporated elements from it—and the principles behind it—into all the other classes I have taught at my university. I also developed a graduate form of the same course (English L-504),[9] distinguished mainly by a more extended—and, yes, *theoretical*—section, in which I wanted students to be able to think creatively about what constitutes a manuscript, as opposed to a printed, allegedly "finished" text. The following examples are drawn mainly from the experiences I have had in my work with undergraduates, since they are the audience probably least familiar with special collections, while graduate students are more likely to have at least an inkling of the importance of materials kept there. Most of my illustrations are drawn from L-460 (in the appendix to this essay, I am including a syllabus for that class), but I will also draw from units that I have used in subsequent classes (such as L-356, Nineteenth-Century American Poetry, and L-317, the second part of the Nineteenth-Century American Literary Survey) and that I continue to use in new classes I develop. This eclectic approach will involve some switching back and forth between the past and the present tense, but I hope the main ideas will remain clear.

■ ■ ■

I had planned L-460 as a small class, with an enrollment limited to fifteen, a classic capstone course within our major and manageable enough for me to work individually with each student (although when the time came, I had to allow additional students to enroll). The course began with a few weeks devoted to the joint study of archives I had selected, ranging from an entire author-based collection—the papers of Sarah Helen Whitman, the one-time fiancée of Edgar Allan Poe and subsequent fierce defender of his reputation—to more focused assignments, such as the various drafts of a chapter from Theodore Dreiser's autobiography, *Dawn* (published in 1931), or Lewis Carroll's correspondence with the illustrator of his novel *Sylvie and Bruno,* Harry Furniss (1854–1925).[10] I put the items on reserve, alerted the students when they were available, and asked them to come into the Lilly's Reading Room to work with them ahead of our next meeting. My classes typically meet on Tuesdays and Thursdays in the Ellison Room of Lilly Library, a wonderful space, complete with a (non-working) fieldstone fireplace, sandblasted fir paneling, and rustic, pegged furniture, which houses the collection of Westerniana assembled by Robert Spurrier Ellison (1875–1945) of Wyoming, a former Vice President of the Midwest Refining Company. Each Friday morning and afternoon, I made myself available in the Reading Room to help students (and to ease the burden on the public service staff). In this fashion, we would look at an unpublished, handmade early volume of poems by Stephen Spender, along with letters by the septuagenarian Sir Stephen attesting to the fact that he had forgotten about this work but that he was pleased to be reminded of it; a letter from the flamboyant actress Florence Deshon to her lover Max Eastman about how, in May 1919, she hopped on a plane at the

Hollywood airfield of Charlie Chaplin's brother and went flying all over Hollywood; and a clipping of an 1879 newspaper interview with Walt Whitman, littered with autograph corrections by Whitman himself, who was angry about being censored by his interviewer and reinserted the adjective "constipated" into a sentence about the unacceptable "sweetness" of contemporary American poetry.[11] In a particularly revelatory session, we deciphered Virginia Woolf's holograph corrections and emendations in the proofs to *Mrs. Dalloway* (1925)—last minute alterations made when Harcourt and Brace had agreed to publish the American version of the novel. Woolf's interventions, which included a typed rewrite of the two crucial pages in the novel describing the suicide of Septimus Warren, created a complex textual situation for the novel, which we now realized exists in at least three different versions: as a manuscript, as a set of corrected proofs and—since her corrections came too late for her own publisher to adopt in full and were often too dense to be deciphered by the American printer—in a British and American printed version.

I also invited members of the Lilly staff to talk about their work, from the Director of the Lilly and its Curator of Manuscripts to the Archivist, the Senior Cataloger, the Conservator, and the Head of Public Services, helping the students to track the journey of a manuscript from acquisition to patron use in the Lilly's Reading Room. My goal during these first few weeks was to impress on students that while manuscripts are important sources (e.g., for the historian, the biographer, the literary critic), they are so much more than simple repositories of useful information. Manuscripts teach us to think of texts or other artifacts not as products but steps in a process that began long before a text—or, in the case of Crone's albums—a photograph was published.

Manuscripts also are physical objects in their own right, written or typed on paper that in turn was created by someone else (even if that someone is an anonymous company), which carries the signs of use by those who wrote on it or handled it. Manuscripts allow us a behind-the-scenes look where none seemed possible; they allow us to risk a glance at stories that might and should have been told but weren't. Lewis Carroll's letters to Harry Furniss are a case in point. Furniss was a well-known artist for *Punch,* and he was able to insist on his own artistic views, even when Carroll's criticism of his work was withering. Carroll's *Sylvie and Bruno* is a fiendishly complicated novel involving multiple, mysteriously linked plots and three different worlds of varying degrees of reality, loosely tied together by the characters, among them most prominently the two siblings Sylvie and Bruno, who are sprites or fairies and who are exposed to all sorts of political intrigue. Furniss had his work cut out for him, and Carroll was not an easy boss. For example, in a letter written on November 24, 1886, he complained that Furniss's sketches, while "very graphic & suggestive," were not on a track towards realizing a "comic result." He disliked Furniss's portrayal of Sylvie, who, to Carroll, looked to be more like fifteen than twelve (Carroll's preferred age for girls). Things got so tense that, in a letter dated August 26, 1889, Carroll announced plans to write an essay on "Authors' Difficulties with Illustrators." He also tried to embarrass Furniss by pointing out that his previous illustrator, John Tenniel, has responded to criticism by quietly redoing the image. Furniss was, by all accounts, not an easy man to get along with, but Carroll's letters do reveal an astonishing amount of micromanaging, especially when he drew illustrations himself to steer Furniss in the right direction. Not that Furniss complied. He pushed back when Carroll's creatures—more uncanny and perverse than simply "naughty"—were simply too weird for a Victorian audience. In class, we considered in detail Carroll's draft sketch for the "changed crocodile" (chapter XVI of the first part of *Sylvie and Bruno*), a crocodile willfully shortened by a character named "the Professor" for the benefit of Sylvie and Bruno and then lengthened again to more than "two times and half its original size," all "just because" (figure 15.1). The flexible crocodile is a great addition to Carroll's unsettling collection of diminishing and expanding bodies, which to many modern critics has suggested some kind of sexual meaning but is certainly also, as William Empson showed long ago, a nifty response to children's natural obsessions with their own size and the size of the world.[12]

    Carroll's serpent-like reptile—which, in Carroll's second drawing on this page, becomes a kind of bizarre Ouroboros—appears tamed in Furniss's rendition, tidied up, nudged into humorously awkward acceptability by the addition of the accouterments of Victorian masculinity (figure 15.2). He is now a suave gentleman about town rather than the exaggerated, prehistoric-looking, vaguely phallic, naked-looking creature recently emerged from the original slime that Carroll had imagined.[13]

Students in the class were divided as to which one was the more effective illustration—the somewhat nightmarish one sprung from Lewis Carroll's subversive mind or its transformation into gnarly adorability by the more audience-conscious Furniss.

Often manuscripts are ravishingly beautiful. I usually like to show my classes a note to the Reverend Everett Hale written, likely in 1856,

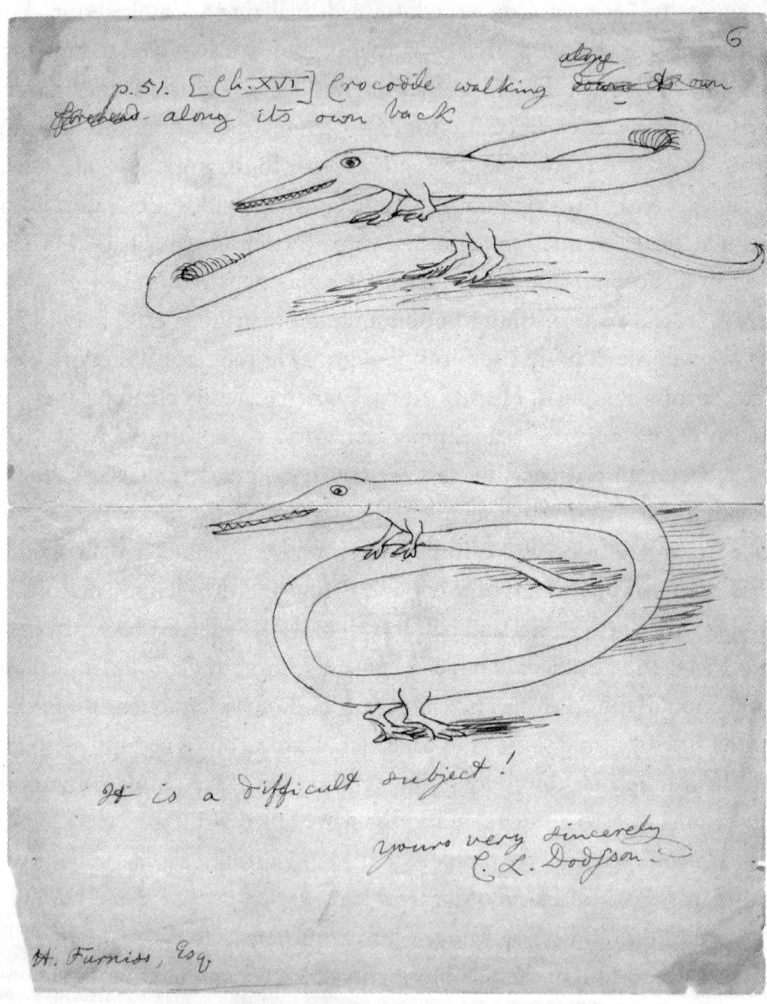

FIGURE 15.1. Lewis Carroll, "Crocodile walking along its own back," letter fragment dated September 1889 [?], Carroll Mss. (courtesy of the Lilly Library, Indiana University Bloomington)

xvi]   A CHANGED CROCODILE.   229

"Oh, but it did though!" Bruno put in eagerly. "It *were* proud of its new tail! Oo never saw a Crocodile so proud! Why, it could go round and walk on the top of its tail, and along its back, all the way to its head!"

"Not *quite* all the way," said Sylvie. "It couldn't, you know."

"Ah, but it *did*, once!" Bruno cried triumphantly. "Oo weren't looking——but *I* watched it. And it walked on tipplety-toe, so as it wouldn't wake itself, 'cause it thought it were asleep. And it got both its paws on its tail. And it walked and it walked all the way along its back. And it walked and it walked on its forehead. And it walked a tiny little way down its nose! There now!"

This was a good deal worse than the last puzzle. Please, dear Child, help again!

FIGURE 15.2. Lewis Carroll, page 229 from *Sylvie and Bruno* (1889), Carroll Mss. (courtesy of The Lilly Library, Indiana University Bloomington)

by the poet Emily Dickinson. My students are invariably surprised by the abstract visual patterns the poet's handwriting created on the page. Barely putting any pressure on her pen, filling every available inch of the paper, writing from margin to margin, she loops and slants her letters as if the impression it would make on the reader were what mattered as much as the content. Which was, as the class agreed, cryptic on its own terms. Dickinson had first written to the Reverend Hale, a minister in Worcester, Massachusetts, in 1854, to inquire how a friend of hers, Benjamin Franklin Newton (a name that one would find only in such a waspy context!), had died and whether or not he had embraced his Savior. The Reverend had written back and somewhat churlishly—from Dickinson's perspective—suggested that she should have rushed to her dying friend's bedside, rather than writing letters after his demise—a suggestion the notoriously reclusive Dickinson, in her miffed response, flatly rejected, since this would have been a pleasure entirely too "costly" for her (figuratively speaking). Two years after her first letter to Hale, she was writing to him again, as if to revisit the debacle of their earlier correspondence, and promised the Reverend that she would "cull" him "buds serener" at some future point in time, namely "upon a purer morn" (figure 15.3). Imagine the poor Reverend's confusion! Was she ironically alluding to the afterlife when they would meet (an afterlife Dickinson did not really believe in, as poems such as "Because I could not Stop for Death" show), and did she combine that facetious promise with the equally ironic—and of course completely inappropriate—prospect of sexual favors granted? The physical appearance of the letter, its pictogrammatic appeal on the page, enhanced the mystery of its promise—a reminder to the good Reverend that Emily Dickinson was not to be measured by conventional standards. What students also got from Dickinson's message was a distinct sense that no transcription of an autograph can ever do justice to the original.[14]

■ ■ ■

During these four or five weeks of joint study, I asked students to investigate and commit to projects that they would then go on to study on their own during the rest of the semester. I met with each member of the class individually and, after inviting them to describe their interests or post-graduation plans, proposed projects to them based on my own

Chapter 15: Teaching with Special Collections

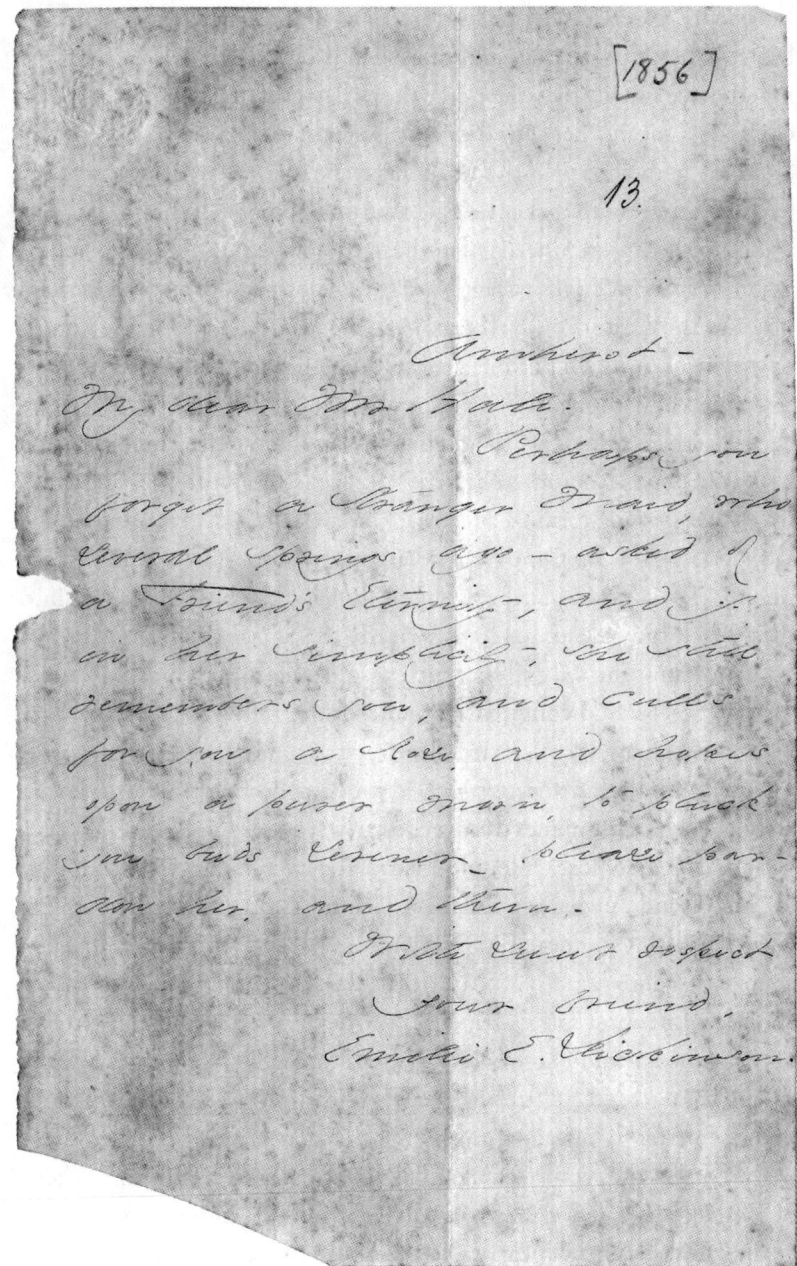

FIGURE 15.3. Emily Dickinson to Everett Edward Hale [1856], American Literature Mss., The Lilly Library (by permission of the Fellows of Harvard College and the Lilly Library, Indiana University Bloomington; © President and Fellows of Harvard College)

knowledge of the Lilly's collections. I would also show them how to browse the Lilly's catalogs and finding aids on their own. The fact that my students usually pick their own projects—both in L-460 and my other classes—means that they develop a sense of ownership towards them. Some students consult with me; others come to me with discoveries they have made or resources that I wasn't aware of. Sometimes they find things by accident: Upton Sinclair's half-hearted application for admission to graduate study in English at Harvard (he was turned down);[15] scripts and notes by the creators of the series *All in the Family* regarding the notorious segment in which Edith nearly becomes the victim of sexual violence that show how thoughtfully they researched and discussed the controversial subject, distancing themselves from contemporary accounts that usually blame the victim;[16] or a series of love letters written in the 1880s by a sailor longing for his fiancée back home as he was travelling on the USS *Enterprise* from Cape Henry, Virginia, to Cape Town, South Africa (figure 15.4). Lt. Mason Abercrombie Shufeldt had poured his soul into these beautifully illustrated letters, clearly out of fear that she might forget about him (she *did* and she married someone else).[17]

The wealth and comprehensiveness of the Lilly's collections makes it easy to find a match for virtually everyone. Thus, Bernadette Patino, a student of Filipino ancestry, delved into a collection of photographic albums of the Philippines during the early years of the American occupation. Anjona Ghosh, a double major in telecommunications and a fan of James Bond movies, looked at Ian Fleming's correspondence with his editor, William Plomer (1903–73), while Becky Ferber, an avid hiker, compared contemporary writer Scott Russell Sanders's journal notes about a whitewater rafting trip with the description of the same trip in his published memoir *Hunting for Hope*.[18] (Sanders, a Bloomington writer who has donated his extensive papers to the Lilly, visited the class later in the semester to talk about how it felt to be "archived.") Elizabeth Pappas, a dyed-in-the-wool Vonnegut fan, looked at the eccentric notes kept by her idol while he was an increasingly rebellious anthropology student at the University of Chicago; she recovered two poems Vonnegut had scribbled on loose-leaf paper in which he was already contemplating one of his favorite themes: "the Grand Ideal, Oblivion/To be shared by all."[19] Erika Jenns read through many of the thirty-plus volumes of journals left

Chapter 15: Teaching with Special Collections

FIGURE 15.4. Cover for Mason Abercrombie Shufeldt, Letter to Elise Buckingham, February 7, 1883, written from Cape Verde; Shufeldt Illustrated Letters, Lilly Mss. (courtesy of The Lilly Library, Indiana University Bloomington)

by Don Belton, a recently deceased faculty member in English, whose entire estate had become the property of the Lilly after he had fallen victim to a violent crime. (Erika went on to also catalog Belton's extensive library for the English Department.)[20] Finally, Deborra Sanders, a student fascinated by the rich Bloomsbury collections of the Lilly, transcribed some of Virginia Woolf's correspondence with her friend Molly McCarthy, paying special attention to her rich metaphorical language, which allowed Deborra to show, in the microcosm of the individual letter, what Bloomsbury as a whole had exemplified: the breaking down of the barriers between art and life.[21]

The Bloomsbury magic had not worked so well for the subject of Michelle Gottschlich's project. Karin Costelloe Stephen (1890–1953), a peripheral member of Woolf's circle and one of the first female psychoanalysts in the United Kingdom, is now mostly remembered because of her marriage to Woolf's brother—unjustly so, as Michelle showed in transcriptions of several key letters from Stephen's career, including several written during her work as a psychiatric resident at Sheppard and Enoch Pratt Hospital in Baltimore, Maryland. Stephen had called the hospital a "grim...fairyland," where she had to assert herself against supercilious male doctors but also seems to have made a real difference in sick people's lives. As she wrote to her mother, Mary Berenson, on October 20, 1927, in a letter transcribed by Michelle:

> I am having exactly the sort of experience now that I could have hoped for in my wildest fancies. I wouldn't have missed this for anything and it amply justifies the trouble of qualifying medically. I have my hands much too full but I could fill them 10 times over with interesting work. I wish I could see you and talk about all this, letters are hopeless to convey experiences of this kind. I feel I am getting much surer about the fundamental underlying drives in human beings and more skill in getting patients to drop their pretences and camouflages and face-savings and recognise what is really true about themselves. It is like being a strange kind of priest but the only doctrine you preach is honesty.[22]

■ ■ ■

I always require students to present their work-in-progress to the entire class. I help them put on reserve, in the Lilly's Reading Room, selections from the material to be prepared and help them post study questions to the course blog. Class members are invited to post their responses to this material either before or after our meetings. Fortunately, I usually don't have any problem finding students willing to present early in the semester—I tell them that they get beneficial peer responses to their work sooner than others. The students also use the blogs I set up to share work-in-progress, to ask questions that come up as they begin to write about their material and, at the end of the semester, to publish the results of their work. So far I have relied on BlogSpot software, since it's simple to navigate and allows for easy posting of diverse materials, including video clips. I am fairly open as to the format students choose for their final projects—submissions have ranged from conventional term papers to elaborate web exhibits. At the end of the semester, all students post to the course blog their finished projects or links to other sites they might have created.

Often, unexpected correspondences and synergies between projects emerge. A good example was the response generated by Bernadette Patino's project on the Frank Crone Mss.: an archive of photographs, speeches, and clippings assembled by the American Director of Education in the Philippines from August 1913 to June 1916.[23] Among the highlights of Bernadette's archive were photographs of the portly Mr. Crone posing next to the corn plants he had taught Filipinos to grow and handing out awards to the most deserving of his corn-growing pupils. Why corn? Being a Hoosier, that's what Crone knew. A particularly poignant example is a photograph featuring a grinning Crone next to General Emilio Aguinaldo (1869–1964), the leader of the Philippine resistance against Spain and the United States and the island's first President until he was captured by American forces in 1901 (figure 15.5).

In her comments on the photograph, Bernadette notes that Crone's caption has stripped Aguinaldo of his military rank. Crone had asked him to stand in front of the corn plot grown by Aguinaldo's son, Emilio Jr., as part of a school project. The former Minister of the Interior on the Philippine Islands, Dean C. Worcester, used the same image as the frontispiece of volume 1 of his anthropological study, *The Philippines: Past and Present* (1914), offering the following assessment in his caption:

Part III: From Periphery to Center

FIGURE 15.5. Frank L. Crone, photographer—"Señor Emilio Aguinaldo, in front of his corn plot, Cavit [sic], Cavite, December 16, 1912. Philippine Islands"; Album #2, Crone Mss. (courtesy of the Lilly Library, Indiana University Bloomington)

"This chance photograph showing General Emilio Aguinaldo as he is to-day... typifies the peace, prosperity, and enlightenment which have been brought about in the Philippine Islands under American rule." In a statement to Committee on the Philippines of the United States Senate delivered in Washington, DC, on December 30, 1914, Worcester used this photograph again and reiterated his justification for the American occupation, praising Aguinaldo's new-found meekness: "I may say that he is more easy to photograph now than he once was.... Aguinaldo does not represent the highest class, although since his surrender he has been a good citizen."[24]

In a response to Bernadette's work posted on the course blog, Ly Nguyen, who had spent the semester reading and transcribing autograph letters by the young James Baldwin,[25] drew parallels between Bernadette's observations about the Philippine occupation and the history of slavery. She provided her own image, a well-known 1841 print by Edward William Clay showing a caring master and his family, surrounded by grateful slaves, a "sacred legacy from my ancestors," as the master helpfully explains.[26] Baldwin, in his early essays, had made a point of excoriating the noxious tradition of white benevolence, blasting even *Uncle Tom's Cabin*—"Everybody's Protest Novel" as he called it—as enmeshed in the logic of racist paternalism.[27] "Like the Americans who wished to educate and civilize the Filipino people," wrote Ly, "pro-slavery advocates also wanted to project the image that they could do good for the people they were colonizing and forcing into slavery." And Ly expanded her argument to make a more general point about the power of images in racist domination: "If one was uninformed about the brutality and dehumanizing reality of slavery... the image [of the master taking care of his slaves] would not seem to be that bad. Everyone in the print looks as if they were enjoying themselves, so what would one object to? The relevance here is Bernadette's point about how Crone and the American officials were the ones who were responsible for the image of the Philippines Americans saw." (Crone went on to use his photographs in lectures he gave about the Philippines after he had returned to the United States.)[28] Ly's comments sharpened Bernadette's narrative in the web exhibit she submitted as her final project, using free Omeka software. Bernadette's exhibit was subsequently added to the Lilly's public website, along with another exhibit developed by Mary Bowden, a student in the graduate version of my class. Mary's "Building Jerusalem in America" re-created the story of an intentional community founded in 1834 in Mount Carmel, Indiana, by working-class emigrants from Manchester.[29]

Of course, I would also accept more traditional essays or written project narratives, as long as students were willing to publish them on the course blog (and as long as they also contained transcriptions of the material the student had consulted). An outstanding example from L-460 was Michelle Gottschlich's paper on Karin Stephen. Michelle is an accomplished poet, and she used her great talent for feeling her way into the minds of other people to make Virginia Woolf's luckless sister-in-law come alive again, at least for the duration of a few pages. It was a joy to see how Michelle immersed herself in the Stephens collection, to an extent that went far beyond the confines of a final research project.

The loving, profoundly moving portrait of Stephen (figure 15.6) that Michelle produced in her final essay will forever be etched in my mind. Instead of a research project, Michelle had written a prose poem:

FIGURE 15.6. Unknown photographer—Karin Stephen at Bryn Mawr, 1908/1909, H. W. Smith Papers, box 18, folder 23 (courtesy of The Lilly Library, Indiana University Bloomington)

a recreation, in lyrical language, of the life of someone who had been on the margins of all the important intellectual movements of her time without ever being allowed to become a fully vested member of any of them. As Michelle wrote (and I have never forgotten these two sentences), "We rarely value the person who lives, and leaves us, as an outsider, and we deny that there is much to learn about history from the periphery. Yet Karin knew these spaces in a way we have lost access to."[30] Stephen was to the manor born, at least culturally and intellectually. Her parents were Frank Costelloe, an English barrister, and Mary Pearsall Smith, the daughter of the writer and suffragist Hannah Whitall. Her stepfather was the famous art historian and critic Bernard Berenson. But although she studied at Cambridge University and Bryn Mawr College and associated with the Bloomsbury group, Karin never fully fit into that tightly woven web of friends, siblings, and lovers. Isolated by her increasing deafness, she valiantly carved out a different space for herself, decades before her sister-in-law demanded that women be given a room of their own. Michelle's re-creation of Karin Stephen (who would eventually commit suicide) drew heavily on her letters, many of which Michelle had laboriously

Chapter 15: Teaching with Special Collections

transcribed in the Lilly's Reading Room. She read Stephen's letters with great sensitivity and an eye for her quiet, unsettling humor, always teetering on the abyss that would finally claim her. I have rarely seen undergraduates weep for reasons other than bad grades—but when Michelle gave her presentation on Stephen, many in the room were visibly moved.

■ ■ ■

The level of excitement in my special collections-based courses is palpable, and I can assure you that the reason for that is not whatever skills I might possess as a teacher. My students are more than ready to embrace special collections materials, to handle them, to study them, to make them part of their lives—and, might I say, they do so with more care and love and respect than many of my more seasoned colleagues. By the time their work is done, *they* are the experts; *they* know more about the artifact or a series of special collections artifacts than I do. In these classes I am a student as well as a professor. They have proved to be a great way of involving students directly in work at a reasonably advanced level, giving them skills that might help them as they are considering careers outside the traditional paths for English majors or PhDs (be it in the field of public history, the National Park Service, or libraries). Three of the seventeen students enrolled in L-460 have gone on to study library science. But for many of my students—as I know from the letters and emails I receive, sometimes years later—the real appeal of these classes cannot be limited to skill sets. Students who have taken my courses know that manuscripts come in all sorts of forms, and they celebrate the diversity they encounter: letters (Florence Deshon, Ian Fleming, Karin Stephen, Bartolomeo Vanzetti, Sarah Helen Whitman, and Virginia Woolf); journals (Belton, Shufeldt, and Woolf); as drafts of shorter or longer texts, such as poems, stories, novels (Dreiser and Belton); in the form of outlines for television shows (*All in the Family*); class notes (Vonnegut); annotations in books and notes on proof sheets (Woolf); and captions in albums (Frank Crone). They may be handwritten or typed or they exist virtually (as the files on Belton's university computer, for example). Manuscripts can be by famous people and by ordinary people; they may be historically important or relevant for understanding a person's life, or both. Or they may touch you on an entirely different, personal level, as happened to

Alicia Scott, who fiercely defended the unlucky Mr. Shufeldt's letters against objections by some classmates that they weren't anything special. The fact that Special Collections is a place where all these voices come alive again—where Vanzetti's voice, silenced by his execution on August 22, 1927, still resonates, and the forgotten Mr. Shufeldt is still allowed to long for his unfaithful fiancée—will help them see not only libraries very differently. My approach has worked if, in the eyes of my students, there is indeed nothing particularly special—in the sense of specialized, remote, or refined—about special collections. For my students, they become a gateway to the world.

ENG-L 460 (Spring 2013)

Modern Literary Archives
Tuesdays and Thursdays, 2:30 PM—3:45 PM
The Ellison Room, The Lilly Library
Christoph Irmscher
www.christophirmscher.com
Office hours: W 3-4 and by appointment

Course description

Have you ever wondered about what it would be like to work not with someone else's edition of a novel, a work of poetry, or a play but with the actual source, the manuscript or typescript handled by the author himself or herself? Have you ever asked yourself how your argument in a term paper might be made stronger by referring to an unpublished letter, an early draft of a poem, an annotated book once owned by your author? Or do you just enjoy spending time in libraries or museums? If any of this applies to you, then this is the course for you. Manuscripts are a literary critic's bread-and-butter; this course will introduce you, in hands-on fashion, to the practical and ethical principles of working with modern literary archives. We will draw exclusively on original materials from the Lilly's collections, from the papers of such outstanding writers as William Wordsworth, John Keats, Edgar Allan Poe, William Carlos Williams, Virginia Woolf, Sylvia Plath, W. Somerset Maugham, Kurt Vonnegut, and others.

Some of the topics and skills to be covered might include the "archeology" of literary texts (i.e., all that comes before the "fair copy" of a manuscript, such as drafts, notebooks, reading notes, and letters); exercises in deciphering handwriting; principles and types of textual transcription; prepublication documents (annotated and fair copies) as well as publication-related documents (page proofs); the nature of the literary archive or collection; the use of finding aids in libraries; and so forth.

Course requirements

This is a practicum in which, after some weeks of introductory conversations, I will assist you in your work. Initially we will meet and do some practical exercises with material I have selected. You are expected to prepare for these meetings carefully by visiting the Lilly regularly. I will make myself available—in the Lilly Reading Room—on most mornings to be on hand to help you. Make sure that you come to class ready to share your notes and/or editions. When you discuss your own work, you are required to make copies of your findings or post the results of your work in advance of the meeting to the course blog.

I will meet with you early in the semester (always at the Lilly) to determine what project you might be interested in. I will ask you to describe your work during the semester in regular, brief updates to be posted to the course website (http://lillymodernarchives.blogspot.com). I expect about 4 in the course of the semester. There is no prescribed length or deadline. Share a problem, an editorial decision you feel you need to make, a discovery, an epiphany or a disappointment you had.

By the end of the course (05/01), I will expect you to have produced a short critical edition of an original manuscript from your field of interest (five to ten pages) using your archive of choice from the Lilly's collections as well as a short essay commenting on the archive and your editorial practice. The essay needs to explain the principle behind your edition, comment on choices you had to make, as well as the opportunities that you see your edition offers. You may choose to present your final edition in traditional print format or as a digital document. There is no textbook for this class. Regular attendance and participation in our meetings as well as posting to the blog count for 30 percent of the grade. Presenting your project to the class will make up another 30 percent; your final project will account for the final 40 percent.

continued on next page

Part III: From Periphery to Center

Week 1

01/08   Introduction: What are manuscripts? Examples of manuscripts.

01/10   Preliminary exercises: Sylvia Plath, "Finisterre" or "The Surgeon at 2 AÂMÂ" (Plath Mss.). I will be available Wednesday morning to help you with the material. Compare the autograph with the printed text and write down what you observe.

Week 2

01/15   An unpublished autograph: Stephen Spender, "Poems Written Abroad." Spender Mss.

Each student should pick one poem from the collection, transcribe it, and post it to the course blog. Don't worry if the same poem is selected by several people. Describe the entire autograph as carefully as possible.

01/17   Spender, cont.

Week 3

01/22   Lewis Carroll, Letters and Drafts for *Sylvie and Bruno*. Additional reading: Kelemen, "Why Study Textual Editing and Criticism?" (course blog)

01/ 24   Multiple Drafts: Theodore Dreiser, *Dawn*

Week 4

01/29   Dreiser, *Dawn*

01/31   From Autograph to Print: Virginia Woolf, *Mrs. Dalloway*

Additional Reading: Erick Kelemen, "Text Technologies and Textual Transmissions" (course blog)

Week 5

02/05   Cherry Williams, Curator of Manuscripts

02/07   *Mrs. Dalloway*, cont.

Week 6

02/12   Working with Archives: Editing the Sarah Helen Whitman Correspondence

02/14   Sarah Helen Whitman, cont.; Visit Craig Simpson, Archivist

continued on next page

Chapter 15: Teaching with Special Collections

Week 7

02/19   Working with Archives: The Florence Deshon Mss.
02/21   Visit Jim Canary, Conservator at the Lilly

Week 8

02/26   Deshon Mss., cont.
02/28   Erika Jenns on the Don Belton Mss.

Week 9

03/05   Michelle Gottschlich on Karin Stephen
03/07   Anjona Ghosh on Ian Fleming; Deborra Sanders on Virginia Woolf

Week 10

03/12 and 03/14 SPRING BREAK

Week 11

03/19   Ava Dickerson on Charles Baudelaire; Bernadette Patino on Frank Crone
03/21   Megan Jones on Sacco and Vanzetti

Week 12

03/26   Ariel Hunt on William Carlos Williams
03/28   Ly Nguyen on James Baldwin

Week 13

04/02   Morgan Burris on Sylvia Plath; Alicia Scott on Mason Shufeldt
04/04   Elizabeth Pappas on Kurt Vonnegut; Steven Whyte on Sarah Helen Whitman

Week 14

04/09   Rebecca Ferber on Scott Russell Sanders
04/11   Instructor on his own project (Audubon)

Week 15

04/16   Visit Scott Russell Sanders
04/18   Audrey Snider on *The Wizard of Oz;* Aaron Denton on Carver

continued on next page

Part III: From Periphery to Center

> **Week 16**
> Individual Meetings with Participants. Definitely no class on Tuesday!
> 04/25   Wrap-up
> 05/01   Submission of Final Version of Project

ACKNOWLEDGMENTS

I would like to thank Joel Silver, Director of the Lilly Library, and Cherry Williams, Curator of Manuscripts at the Lilly Library, for reading this essay and for the permission to use materials from their collection. Leslie Morris, Curator of Modern Books and Manuscript at Harvard University's Houghton Library, graciously gave me permission to use Emily Dickinson's letter to Edward Everett Hale. Thanks also to my former students Michelle Gottschlich, Megan Jones, Ly Nguyen, and Bernadette Patino for allowing me to quote from their work. All images were taken by Zach Downey.

NOTES

1. Bartolomeo Vanzetti to Mary Donovan, December 28, 1926, Hapgood Mss., Sacco-Vanzetti Papers, The Lilly Library.
2. One of the epigraphs taken from "Puddn'head Wilson's Calendar" in Mark Twain's novel *Puddn'head Wilson,* originally published in 1894 (New York: Pocket Books, 2004), 179.
3. Nicola Sacco and Bartolomeo Vanzetti, *The Letters of Sacco and Vanzetti,* ed. Gardner Jackson and Marion Frankfurter (1928; New York: Penguin Books, 2007), 164–65; Megan Jones, "Vanzetti's Voice: A Critical Look at the Letters of Bartolomeo Vanzetti," Honors Thesis, English, submitted April 4, 2014, Indiana University Bloomington, English Department, 48. Megan, now at the University of Kansas, and I are collaborating on a new edition of the Vanzetti letters.
4. Mary Donovan married the labor leader and union organizer Powers Hapgood on December 28, 1927.
5. Hapgood Mss., Sacco-Vanzetti Papers, box labeled "Printed," folder "Broadsides & Armband," The Lilly Library.
6. See the chapter on "The Rise of English" in Terry Eagleton, *Literary Theory: An Introduction* (Oxford: Blackwell, 1983).
7. See Ezra Pound, *ABC of Reading* (London: Faber, 1961) 17–18.

8. John H. Overholt, "Five Theses on the Future of Special Collections," *RBM: A Journal of Rare Books, Manuscripts, and Cultural Heritage* 14.1 (2013): 15–20,. http://nrs.harvard.edu/urn-3:HUL.InstRepos:10601790.
9. The blog for the graduate version of the class can be found at www.lillymanuscripts.blogspot.com (access by permission).
10. Dreiser Mss., box 1, The Lilly Library; Carroll Mss., The Lilly Library.
11. Stephen Spender, "Poems Written Abroad" (1927), English Literature Mss., The Lilly Library, and Spender to John Yarnall, August 4, 1964, Lilly Library Administrative Files; Florence Deshon to Max Eastman, March 9, 1920, Deshon Mss., The Lilly Library; "Walt Whitman in St. Louis. Literature, Politics, and the Prairie States. Two Manuscript Notes and Printed Newspaper Clipping, with Holograph Additions by Whitman," The Lilly Library, Manuscripts PS 3222.W62 1879.
12. William Empson, "The Child as Swain," *Some Version of Pastoral* (New York: New Directions, 1950); see especially 266–67.
13. For more on Furniss and his exceedingly difficult relationship with Carroll, see *Lewis Carroll & His Illustrators: Collaborations & Correspondence, 1865–1898*, ed. Morton N. Cohen and Edward Wakeling (Ithaca, NY: Cornell University Press, 2003), 100–107.
14. Emily Dickinson to Everett Hale, January 13, 1854 and 1856 [?], American Literature Mss., The Lilly Library. Dickinson's response to Hale's letter, dated February 14, 1854, is at the Frost Library of Amherst College and was published in Diana Wagner and Marcy Tanter, "New Dickinson Letter Clarifies Hale Correspondence," *The Emily Dickinson Journal* VII.1 (1998): 110–17.
15. Sinclair Mss. V, The Lilly Library.
16. The episode in question was "Edith's Fiftieth Birthday," aired originally on October 16, 1977. *All in the Family* Mss., The Lilly Library, Box 1, 0805 Box 1. See especially the notes on the Writer's meetings, August 23, 26, 31, 1977.
17. Mason Abercrombie Shufeldt, 1852–1892. Illustrated letters, 1882–1883, Lilly Mss., The Lilly Library. See www.indiana.edu/~liblilly/blog/sailor/.
18. William Plomer Mss. II, The Lilly Library; Scott Russell Sanders, Journal, June 9 to 13, 1995, Scott Russell Sanders Mss., box 9, The Lilly Library.
19. Kurt Vonnegut, "Matter can neither be created nor destroyed…" (1946), Vonnegut Mss., box 21, folder labeled "Anthropology 220."
20. See the Don Cornelius Belton Mss., boxes 1–3. Erika Jenns's website devoted to Belton can be found at http://belton.indiana.edu/~belton/collection/about. For more on Belton, see https://justicefordonbelton.wordpress.com.
21. Virginia Stephen (later Woolf) to Molly McCarthy, March 1912 and undated [1923], The Molly McCarthy Mss., The Lilly Library.
22. Karin Stephen to Mary Berenson, October 20, 1927, Correspondence, Stephen, 1927, May–December, box 12, H. Whitall Smith Manuscripts, The Lilly Library.
23. Bernadette Patino, "Documenting Empire: Frank L. Crone's Photographs of the Colonial Philippines," www.indiana.edu/~liblilly/digital/exhibitions/exhibits/show/

crone. Bernadette now works as a writer for the Film Development Council of the Philippines.
24. "Statement of the Hon. Dean C. Worcester, Formerly a Member of the Philippine Commission," *Hearings before the Committee on the Philippines of the United States Senate, Sixty-Third Congress, Third Session on H.R. 18459, Part 4* (Washington, DC: Government Printing Office, 1915), 272.
25. Baldwin Mss., The Lilly Library.
26. See the image archived by the Library of Congress at www.loc.gov/pictures/resource/pga.05677/.
27. James Baldwin, "Everybody's Protest Novel" (1949), in Baldwin, *Notes of a Native Son* (1955: Boston: Beacon, 2012) 13–24.
28. Ly Nguyen, "Education as Rhetoric of Colonization," March 20, 2013, http://lillymodernarchives.blogspot.com/2013/03/education-as-rhetoric-of-colonization.html (access by permission).
29. Mary Bowden, "Building Jerusalem in America: William Ashton and a Trans-Atlantic Utopia," www.indiana.edu/~liblilly/digital/exhibitions/exhibits/show/ashton. These and other exhibits are discussed in a recent article about Omeka use in the display of Library collections, Juliet L. Hardesty, "Exhibiting Library Collections Online: Omeka in Context." *New Library World* 115, no. 3/4 (2014): 75–86.
30. Michelle Gottschlich, "Recovering Karin Stephen," unpublished essay (2013).

CHAPTER 16

From Siberia to Shangri-La

SARAH THOMAS

Special collections were once marginalized. At one university where they occupied a windowless underground space, they were known as Siberia because it was where people who were problematic—who were surly and unfriendly or unproductive or unable to adjust to the digital world—were exiled. Special collections had many rules, and they were alien and off-putting. There were many hurdles to jump before gaining admittance. Even well-established, serious researchers—such as the head of a special collections division at a large Midwestern university library— were required to submit documentation of their purpose and testimonials to their character. Undergraduates and even graduate students might be rebuffed in their requests to see manuscripts or other materials, with directions to use a microfilm or other surrogate, rather than being allowed to see an original. The rules were intimidating to the uninitiated. A novice visitor might be scolded for bringing a pen into the reading room, not understanding that only pencils were allowed because of the potential of ink to mar a page. Unlike libraries serving general collections, where there were open stacks for browsing and consultation, rare book and special collections required users to request items in advance, and they had to be fetched from locked areas, a task that often required hours or even days. Many collections were uncataloged, so even when potential users knew the archive of a particular writer or entity had been acquired, even with great fanfare, the holdings remained inaccessible, often in the cartons in which they had arrived. Processing collections could take years, and many acquisitions remained boxed and untouched indefinitely. Regulars received favored treatment, or so it seemed, while the uninitiated struggled to navigate the unfamiliar bureaucracy. Hours were short. Libraries opened at 9:00 or 10:00 and closed at 5:00, Monday through Friday; evening and weekend hours were few and far between. White glove treatment prevailed. Special collections were treasures to be protected, the purview of the scholarly elite.

As general collections became more uniform, more easily shared, and thus more accessible, there was a heightened awareness of the value of primary sources and unique and distinctive collections. In 1998, the Association of Research Libraries (ARL) surveyed its member libraries on the status of their special collections, with the objective of examining the role of special collections in teaching and learning; exploring the way digitization was increasing access; determining the condition of the large body of nineteenth-century holdings; and understanding the potential for libraries and other cultural heritage organizations that might collaborate to integrate access to documents held separately in many institutions.[1]

The ARL report noted that many special collections had not been processed; that staffing was insufficient to support increasing demand for teaching and other forms of outreach; that library collection policies often did not reference special collections; and preservation remained an unfunded mandate.

In the US, by 2008, the Andrew W. Mellon Foundation, which had generously supported the digitization and cataloging of individual collections for over a decade, had worked with the Council on Library and Information Resources (CLIR) to establish the Hidden Collections cataloging program, with a seven-year initiative to award $23.5 million to a diverse group of US repositories by the end of 2014. The goal was to bring collections of scholarly importance that were languishing in boxes and backlogs into the light through supporting the creation of finding aids and bibliographic records according to innovative and standard practices. The accomplishments of this program have been massive; people have not only uncovered buried treasure, but they have discovered new approaches to increase the yield on the Mellon/CLIR investment.

Christa Williford, Director of Research and Assessment, CLIR, described in her blog some of the advances made through the exploration of proposals to open up collections using new technologies and workflows. In April 2014, she noted:

> Over time, we've observed several trends affecting the cultural heritage institutions that have participated in Hidden Collections: the adoption of "more product/less process" attitudes about maximizing efficiency; the engagement of students, scholars or other non-professionals in the production and assessment of collection descriptions; [and] an explosion in the creative use of social media.[2]

For example, the University of Pennsylvania's Provenance Project used Flickr to invite others to fill in information about provenance using crowdsourcing, and Brown University employed data visualization to express the geographic locations represented in the Gordon Hall and Grace Hoag Collection of Dissenting and Extremist Propaganda.

While I was in the United Kingdom, I was involved in a similar study undertaken by Research Libraries UK (RLUK) and OCLC. RLUK subsequently issued a report in 2014 in which a survey documented that over 13 million volumes in UK research libraries and archives were uncataloged; the problem was especially acute in museums and independent libraries; archival collections were more likely to be hidden than printed materials; the addition of contemporary holdings to backlogs was acerbating the problem; and foreign materials and specialized formats were more likely to be inaccessible.[3]

Librarians are aware of the problem and are actively trying to tackle the backlogs; over 60 percent have retrospective cataloging projects under way. However, the scale of the problem is often beyond individual institutions. Respondents support an online registry of retrospective cataloging and are interested in exploring national initiatives and technical solutions to bring this about.

When contemplating the scale of the enterprise, one wonders, if even the techniques developed in the CLIR Mellon Hidden Collections activities will enable repositories to eliminate backlogs.

There is a shift in the approach to managing unique and distinctive collections in which the hoarder mentality is being given de-cluttering therapy. Or call it the Collyer Brothers meet Open Access. Librarians and archivists are focusing on how to make collections more widely available for use. Although they are not shirking their responsibility to preserve, they are giving deeper consideration to access and they are expanding their notion of whom they serve from a narrow definition of researchers to a broader audience, including the general public.

One approach to increase access has been to insist that an integral element of collection management is that every collection acquired be accompanied by a commitment to process it in a timely manner. My Bodleian colleague Richard Ovenden, then Keeper of Special Collections, now Bodley's Librarian, set a standard of raising or earmarking funds to process collections whenever a new acquisition was completed. This often entailed fund-raising not only to acquire collections, but also for funds for conservation, processing, digitization, and exhibition. The ways in which libraries have become increasingly entrepreneurial to support acquisitions and other aspects of the modern special collections libraries would be another talk unto itself, but they reflect the way in which bookish librarians have transformed themselves into charismatic impresarios, enticing both wider audiences and benefactors to support a cycle of learning and growth.

At the Schlesinger Library at Harvard's Radcliffe Institute for Advanced Study, staff have just completed a five-year initiative to describe all collections that had formed a significant arrearage. Marilyn Dunn, the Executive Director of the Schlesinger Library, courageously organized an approach in which targets to complete processing were set, and staff needed to come up with a plan that would achieve the desired results. The maximum access project, which received funding from the Radcliffe Institute, rose out of the Library's strategic plan in 2007, and became a bold initiative to eliminate the current backlog, a goal that was attained and celebrated in 2013, resulting in the cataloging of the entire print backlog (12,497 titles in addition to 17,675 volumes currently received), in the processing of 207 manuscript collections (6412.49 linear ft., or 80 percent of the manuscript backlog), and in the processing of 8,479 unpublished audiovisual items (or 60 percent of the audiovisual backlog).

The results were impressive in terms of important content made accessible, including a 1778 manumission of a female slave named Elizabeth; spirit writings in chalk dating from spiritualist meetings in the early twentieth-century; the records of a number of national organizations: Lamaze, the National Abortion Rights Action League, Fishermen's Wives of Gloucester (Mass.) Association, Mautner Project for Lesbians with Cancer, documents pertaining to the lives of transgender individuals as well as women who were active in the Republican Party, the papers of National Organization for Women activists; singer Holly Near; and sex educator Shere Hite.

Although supplementary funding enabled the Schlesinger to tackle what would have been impossible to achieve by the existing staff, the demands for productivity were intense. Processors needed to cut their pattern to the cloth; this was not business as usual. Notice the focus on "maximum access" to the Collections, rather than on minimal-level cataloging. The emphasis on the positive aspect of opening up these fascinating documents highlights the importance of providing access in a flexible manner, rather than rigid adherence to uniform application of detailed rules to all documents.

Recently National Public Radio featured a program on an activity at the Smithsonian Institution that encourages the public to transcribe handwritten field notes, logbooks, and diaries. The initiative, which has been a pilot for a year, lays out the methodology and goals in clear language. Smithsonian Digital Volunteers are invited to participate in the transcription, and simple bar graphs inform the viewer of the percent of transcription completed for a given document and how many people are working on it. A brief description of the manuscript sets its chronological frame and offers a short summary of its contents. The work of contributors is showcased in a running commentary of progress made, which cites individual accomplishments.

New applications of technology, coupled with human intelligence and expertise, offer the prospect of circumventing the barriers that have inhibited access to the whole of human knowledge, even as they have been acting in the service of access to a limited number of documents. For example, Harvard's Schlesinger Library is reversing the process for making materials available. Instead of organizing archival collections into folders and series and creating a finding aid, after which the contents might or might not be digitized, the Schlesinger is digitizing first and using a combination of text mining and human intervention to provide access to the content. It is also exploring the use of a program called MONK, a pattern recognition and machine-learning application that is facilitating the conversion of handwritten documents to text while learning to recognize the scripts of individuals.

The next Mellon/CLIR cycle will support digitization, rather than focusing on processing.

With hundreds of unprocessed collections here at Harvard, and increased demand for digital access, what are our options? If we are able to process our printed collections by taking advantage of technological advances and new approaches, we can shift resources to increasing access to our manuscripts, maps, photographs, audiovisual, and other unique and distinctive holdings. We can use crowdsourcing and social media to enrich the data we provide.

Assumptions about the need for description of a particular kind are being challenged. Creative people will consume content in ways hitherto unimaginable. Look, for example, at California artist David Normal's use of the British Library's materials. About a year ago the British Library uploaded over a million images from its nineteenth-century digitized books onto Flickr Commons, inviting consumers to use the images freely. To its surprise Normal, who weaves nineteenth-century illustrations into his paintings, created four megascale works exhibited at the Burning Man festival in Nevada. I particularly enjoyed learning about how the connection was made in this FAQ on the BL site:

> *How did you come across the British Library's Flickr Commons collection?*
>
> The guitarist of the punk band "Flipper" mentioned something about it and at the time I had already initiated the plan to create paintings based on 19th Century images for Burning Man, and so learning of this vast online collection was thrilling and truly fortuitous since it was exactly what I was looking for.[4]

Normal goes on to say:

> Another thing that was very helpful to me was the randomness. The majority of the images are in no particular order in the photostream,

and viewing the images in succession was like taking a journey through a landscape of illustrated symbols.[5]

This openness is aided by policies that allow noncommercial reuse without the need to seek permission, a new practice which has unthrottled creative work. Cornell's policy from 2009 is an example; I am pleased to say that Harvard announced a similar policy as part of Open Access week. The rapid emergence of new applications will characterize the coming years in Special Collections and will revolutionize our understanding of the past and provide new insights for the future.

At the same time this revolution is occurring with digital objects, there are parallel developments in the experience of those encountering original artifacts. In a world of endless reproductions, including amazingly faithful copies, there is a yearning for and fascination with authenticity and the compelling nature of the three-dimensional objects. A pox upon the houses of those who think, "Close all the libraries and buy everyone an Amazon Kindle subscription."[6]

Exhibitions of special collections are attracting larger and larger audiences. The Bodleian had a display of items relating to Mary Wollstonecraft and Percy Bysshe Shelley, "Shelley's Ghost," which brought in approximately 50,000 visitors in a few months. It travelled to New York, and with more daring and popular marketing, it became a destination for many more thousands. Further afield, Australia's Victoria State Library presented a visually enchanting exhibition of the Bodleian's Mughal paintings and manuscripts; opened it with bare-chested flame swallowers, dancing maidens, and musicians; and brought in over 100,000 visitors in less than six months. Personally, I dream of pop-up displays of materials from our libraries in public spaces like Grand Central or Fenway Park.

Even closer to home, this hunger for an understanding of the relationship between form and content, the excitement of simply touching something that changed the direction of history or thought, and the appreciation of the intrinsic aesthetic of a book or map or other document, is driving new courses and engaging the study of special collections within our libraries. At Cornell, this was already a part of the program in the 1990s, when the Kroch Library opened. With user spaces, staff offices, a seminar room, and a small lecture theater encircling an exhibition gallery, it was amazingly forward in its design. And I remember Mark Dimunation enthralling stocky farm boys on a school excursion from a neighboring rural community with slave manacles and the Gettysburg Address. They wrote thank-you notes in their childish script: "Your work is awesome!" More recently, the renovation of the New Bodleian Library, which transformed it from an ugly duckling into a swan, provides copious gallery space for the thousands of tourists who throng Oxford's streets. Above level it is a paradise for readers, perhaps the Shangri-La, the mythical, mystical world of *Lost Horizons*. On the first day readers could enter the building, which had been closed for three years, an academic sent me this enthusiastic note: "I have to say that I think this is one of the biggest steps forward for humanities research we've ever had; it is visible, is a statement of serious intent, and it suggests that we welcome others as well."[7]

This conference brings together a number of the leading practitioners in the area of special collections. I'm acutely conscious of being an administrator amidst you. There are so many topics on which I have not touched that I hope will be reflected in the talks over the next twenty-four hours. There are the themes of acquisitions and fundraising, and of the relationships with collectors, for example, as well as much more to say about new developments in teaching and learning. One needs a much deeper understanding of the nuances of collections.

But if I were to concentrate my thinking into a few sentences, I would say: special collections were once marginal and elitist; now they are at the heart of what we do and they are opening and welcoming. This means that the wonders once enjoyed by a few can now benefit the many. Practices that developed out of the necessities and limitations of the analog age are being superseded by new approaches that combine mass digitization and technological applications to open up collections on a scale hitherto unimaginable. We are moving from a largely text-based environment to one in which all forms of media receive attention. These trends bring new audiences and actors and new uses for materials. They change the nature of our staffing and our space, inviting outward-looking partnerships and interactive environments. As we move from individuals who have worked in a more solitary fashion to teams of people engaging in collective action, so are our institutions shifting emphasis from site-specific to global horizons. Now, no one would characterize special collections as Siberia;

it's that wonderful peak we all hope to scale, with earthly delights and spiritual rewards awaiting us.

NOTES

1. Judith M. Panitch, *Special Collections in ARL Libraries: Results of the 1998 Survey Sponsored by the ARL Research Collections Committee* (Washington, DC: Association of Research Libraries, 2001), www.arl.org/storage/documents/publications/special-collections-arl-libraries.pdf.
2. Christa Williford, "Un-Hidden Collections: CLIR's Seven-Year Experiment in Exposing Scholarly Resources and the Question of Digitization," *CLIR Connect Blog*, April 22, 2014, http://connect.clir.org/blogs/christa-williford/2014/04/22/un-hidden-collections.
3. Caroline Peach and Mike Mertens, eds., *Unique and Distinctive Collections: Opportunities for Research Libraries; a Report by RLUK, Based on Fieldwork Carried Out by Alison Cullingford* (London: Research Libraries UK, 2014), www.rluk.ac.uk/wp-content/uploads/2014/12/RLUK-UDC-Report.pdf.
4. David Normal (edited by Sophie McIvor and Mahendra Mahey and posted on behalf of David Normal), "The British Library Meets Burning Man," *Digital Scholarship Blog*, August 27, 2014, http://britishlibrary.typepad.co.uk/digital-scholarship/2014/08/the-british-library-meets-burning-man.html.
5. Ibid.
6. Tim Worstall, "Close All the Libraries and Buy Everyone an Amazon Kindle Subscription," *Opinion Blog, Forbes*, July 18, 2014. www.forbes.com/sites/tim worstall/2014/07/18/close-the-libraries-and-buy-everyone-an-amazon-kindle-unlimited-subscription/.
7. Private email.

CHAPTER 17

The Once and Future Special Collections

MARK DIMUNATION

I begin with a modern fable, one that is often cited, and that has, as any good fable should, a lesson to be learned.

Dr. Einstein Takes the Train

As the train left the station from Princeton, Albert Einstein was comfortably ensconced in his seat, reading, when he was approached by the conductor with the inevitable request for his ticket. The good doctor responded as one would expect—startled, absent-minded, and a bit flustered. He began to pat down his coat pockets, ruffle through his papers, and survey the area. "It's all right, Dr. Einstein," the conductor offered. "I will finish the train and get your ticket on the way back." When the conductor returned, he found a disheveled Einstein frantically fluttering through his brief case, papers and books askew. The conductor interrupted in a calm and soothing tone. "Dr. Einstein, it is alright. You take the train all the time. Just relax and look for your ticket. I will come by later." Some time had passed. As the conductor returned he found the desperate professor on his hands and knees, his suitcases wide open and clothing flung in all directions. Einstein looked up wide-eyed and terrorized. "Please Dr. Einstein, don't worry. I am sure you will find your ticket." "My dear boy," Einstein sputtered, "it is no longer a question of where is my ticket. It is a question of where am I going."

Well, if Dr. Einstein's predicament feels familiar to those of us in the room, it may very well be because we have all, from time to time, kept our eye on the ticket, while losing track of our destination—minding the solution at the expense of the goal.

It is a tall and impossible order that the organizers of the colloquium upon which this chapter is based set for me: to take a look at what we have learned from the past, to identify what we need to change to advance the value of special collections materials, to ascertain how we can expand access to materials in new formats, and to identify the most significant obstacles and the most promising solutions for the next few years, and perhaps the decades, to come.

Special collections librarians have certainly explored such issues before, this pulse taking of the state of special collections. As a profession we have been remarkably diligent in vetting our work, our image, and our viability against the backdrop of prevailing expectations and attitudes. This penchant for self-examination grew as the profession consolidated and as special collections stepped forward into the vision of a larger audience. Although earlier RBMS preconferences were comfortably didactic and curatorial in orientation, at the very first Association of College and Research Libraries' Rare Book and Manuscripts Section (RBMS) Preconference in 1959 there was a session that explored "Acquainting the Public with Rare Books." However, by and large the next several decades of conferences looked inward at the tasks of the profession: "Collecting Scientific Literature," "The Care of Rare Books," or "Western Americana." By 1967 we began to examine our relationship with the larger library in a program entitled "Techniques of Rare Books." Tucked into the ending of the twenty-first RBMS Preconference in 1980, with its theme of "Books and Society in History," was a fateful workshop entitled "Computers and Rare Books: An Introductory Session." Things changed, it seemed. Suddenly the topics that filled our annual roster for discussion involved outward forces such as funding concerns, strategies, and pressures, which prompted sessions such as "The Twilight of Rare Book Collecting, or How to Stop Worrying and Love Automation," and the 1983 RBMS Preconference theme "Enemies of Books: Revisited."

I entered the profession the following year. From my vantage point we have always as a profession deliberated the future forecast of special collections. Universities were changing, libraries were evolving, technologies were encroaching. Our consideration moved outward. In 1987, the RBMS Preconference theme was "Reconsidering Libraries and Scholarship: Special Collections and New Directions in Humanities Research." The 1990s buzzed with the consideration of "Issues, Strategies and Opportunities" (1990), "Scholarly Communication and the Future of Special Collections (1992)," and the straightforward question in 1993 "Mainstream or Margin? How Others View Special Collections." Our professional literature addressed the politics of building collections. In 1996 the theme was "Getting There From Here: Setting the Agenda for Special Collections in the 21st Century," and by 2002 the theme of the forty-third preconference was "New Occasions, New Duties: Changing Roles and Expectations."

By and large this self-exploration has made us a flexible and forward-looking group, but there have been times when we have become so preoccupied with sussing out specific problems and solutions that we missed the next right thing.

Very few of us, for example, really predicted the degree to which the digital realm would permeate our daily activities and choices. When first confronted, we responded cautiously about the use of our materials in certain technical operations and naturally turned to the old, protective model of guarding the release of images of our materials. And while the fear that digital images would somehow dilute the usefulness of the material object was a short-lived one, it nevertheless did spring from a much stronger professional catechism that we guard the collections from overexposure, and that the justification of our operations would weaken if we somehow relinquished total control of the object in all of its manifestations. We were, simply put, being good stewards. The initial fears expressed by some in the early days of digitization—that we were diminishing the value of our special collections by creating a false surrogate, trafficking that which was unique about our collections—now seems a guarded posture from light years ago, one that would certainly be contraindicated in today's world of near-universal access via the Internet and an army of mobile wireless objects. We soon embraced digitization as an approach to make special collections materials accessible to a larger research constituency. Today, the axiom pushes even further—if you digitize it, they will come. It was because of our impulse as a profession to reassess continually the nature of our operations that we were able relatively quickly to embrace the forest of the digital world rather than attacking the trees. Increasingly, special collections have become a draw in a world in which more and more researchers stay home.

Although for some of us it feels as if an entire career has passed, it was only thirteen years ago that a group of library directors and special collections librarians gathered at Brown University to explore our understanding of the role of special collections in the research library setting. It was one of those landmark meetings. We all walked away with a sense that our ideas had been heard and with a fairly ambitious agenda tucked under our arms. And while it showed promise—especially for the curators and archivists in the crowd—I don't think we imagined that only a few years later we would be at the forefront of conversations regarding more product and less process, options for minimal catalog description, how to create access for hidden collections, and how best to cope with born-digital materials. The fact that today we are addressing issues such as "collaborative strategies to build cross-institutional collections," and exploring special collections as vehicles for outreach and the provision of content, simply indicates that special collections have moved to the center of the research experience.

From the perspective of those of us in the field for many years, what evolved over the past few decades is in essence a new profession. To some degree our objectives remain related to the past; the fundamental nature of our profession, after all, remains the same—to collect, protect, and interpret—but the text and the context are entirely revamped. Here are some of the hard won lessons that we carry forward into the future—attributes and attitudes from our work that will inform the intrinsic nature of special collections in the future. These will not be a surprise; we have been talking about them for decades.

1. Respond to the Academic Program

First, we understand that our collections must respond to the academic program: it is no longer the case that the value of special collections and archives stands on the rarity, completeness, or quality of the collection alone. If our operation is to remain viable in the modern research library, then our collections must address the research needs of the academic program. This we have accomplished through a variety of tactics. We have learned to ask new questions of old sources—gastronomy collections can offer a glimpse into the daily life of Renaissance women, school grammars can be mined to expose the race and gender expectations of a culture, working with scrapbooks and college archives offers ideal classroom experience in researching primary sources.

We have also learned to edit our collection development practices. There are only a few operations extant that can continue to build on a collection strength purely for the sake of the collection alone, without consideration of its applicability to current research. "How the collection will be used" has become an important factor in the conversation regarding acquisitions. Elsewhere in this book, Jay Satterfield's example about purchasing to fill out teaching packets follows this dictum (see chapter 14). Certainly this has guided what is perhaps one of the more exciting recent developments in our acquisition practices. Creative, vital, innovative collections are brought forward in conjunction with the development of academic programs. One need only recall the excitement engendered by Cornell's highly successful effort to document hip hop music and build an entire program of academic course offerings around it to understand the advantages of this model. Alice Schreyer's discussion in chapter 9 of this book about Michael Lang's collection sparking a renewed programmatic response is another good example. In a less involved fashion, there are collections of cowboy novels, zines, handbills, posters, sound recordings, and other numerous new collections that are emerging to respond to changes in academic discourse.

2. Bring the Collection to the User

In 2010, OCLC released its research survey of special collections and archives. In *Taking Our Pulse: The OCLC Research Survey of Special Collections and Archives,*[1] Jackie Dooley and Katherine Luce analyzed survey data that offered a variety of snapshots of the field—some predictable, with the only surprising element in the discussion about making collections accessible through digitization was the strength of the conviction expressed—"user demand for digitized collections remains insatiable."[2] There is no question that the powerful impact of pulling the curtain back on collections previously hidden is that the results sparked a desire to see even more. And with this exciting work coinciding with the current scholarly trend toward examining material culture and nontraditional sources, it clearly signaled that another strong bridge was being built among special collections and archives and the research community. Much exciting and innovative work has been accomplished of late, easily witnessed in the projects supported by the Council on Library and Information Resources' (CLIR) Cataloging Hidden Special Collections and Archives program, funded by the Mellon Foundation, and now being revised to consider digitization.

Projects from all stripes of institutions have processed and documented extraordinary holdings relevant to today's user community, such as Islamic manuscripts at the University of Michigan,[3] the Moravian community as documented at Lehigh University,[4] the Newberry Library's French pamphlet collection,[5] the field books and expedition journals at the Smithsonian,[6] the Mexican American Labor collections at Arizona State,[7] and the Litchfield Historical Society's Revolutionary era collections.[8]

Hidden collections have also served as the locus for collaboration within and amongst institutions. For example:

- PACSCL, the Philadelphia Area Consortium of Special Collections Libraries, launched a highly successful collaborative consortial project for processing and cataloging.
- The Council on Library and Information Resources (CLIR) guided individual proposals to process collections that documented the civil rights and voter education movements in the United States, and merged those projects together into one large collaborative effort so that Emory University's Woodruff Library and Tulane's Amistad Research Center received a single substantial grant for their efforts.
- Yale University and Stanford University joined forces to work on their collections on song, speech, and dance that are held in their recorded sound archives.

- The Black Metropolis Research Consortium brought together 150 Chicago-area collections banded together to address their unprocessed and inaccessible collections documenting the political, cultural, social, spiritual, and economic aspects of African Americans' lives throughout the history of Chicago.

There is a long list of such collaborative ventures. Some will stand as triumphs of innovation in processing, cataloging techniques, and the implementation of technology. There is much we can learn from what has already been achieved. As I perused the proposals and the lists of projects carried out over the past decade, I began to place these accomplishments in the context of what had originally launched our discussions about Hidden Collections. I have been swimming in the waters of these discussions for over ten years now—as an original member of the ARL Special Collections Task Force, as the host of the 2003 Library of Congress Hidden Collections Conference, and as a member of the CLIR Board of Directors. While I am optimistic that our efforts over the years have yielded positive results, I fear that we have been pushed off course and derailed the initial impetus toward a holistic, national rethinking of how we process and make accessible our collections for our constituencies. We have been caught in what Sarah Thomas referred to in chapter 16 of this book as "boutique projects." The Google Books project certainly distracted us from our original concept, and the HathiTrust formula is a pale alternative. Nonetheless, digitization is with us as a dramatic reality, and we will work to make the best of it.

3. Be Exceptional, Not the Exception

Special collection materials are often set out at the forefront of a library's and university's campaigns. We typically care for what is most dramatic and unique within a university's holdings, and so our collections are often enlisted to help the university establish its cachet and its brand. We have learned, however, that just because the university likes our materials does not mean it shares our agenda. If we really believe that special collections are at the heart of the research library, then we need to play on the entire field. We need to be defenders of the faith without the rigidity of righteousness. "Special" can also be a lonely place, and sometimes it means just being the exception. To avoid this fate, however, many of us have learned that we need to understand, support, and participate in larger library-wide initiatives, policies, and procedures. It is better to weigh in on library-wide policy committees and work with other units than to be set aside, or (even worse) to be dismissed as problematic.

We also face what I call the erosion factor. With each embrace of new technology, with each revision of standards and practice, and with each successive wave of innovation, a bit more of our legacy data is washed away. Special collections, archival materials, and nonbook formats were often set off to the side as exceptions when large-scale conversions of bibliographic records were undertaken. The echoes of the promise to return later to create that data grow increasingly faint, and these backlogs remain as our energies and attention are drawn elsewhere. And while this is understandable in some fields where current publications are at a premium, it is a poor model for coping with research-level collections. Before we get too far into trumpeting the twenty-first century, it might behoove us to at least complete the work of the twentieth century.

Of course I am not suggesting here the unrealistic plan of a level 3 retrospective conversion of all outstanding special collections records. At this point we frankly have neither the money nor the capacity for that process. However, I would like us to look at techniques that at least bring the data forward so that all boats can rise with the tide. The failure to do so is a gross disservice to our constituencies and will ultimately undermine our efforts to advance our delivery of information to the modern user. This is not something that can be addressed on a project-by-project approach. It will require an all-out effort to bring it forward.

Similarly, many special collections units were bypassed when library-wide circulation and inventory structures were installed—again because of the unusual manner in which our materials are circulated and housed. It is a lesson hard-learned in some cases, but we understand that as principal players in the research continuum, we need to be vocal and insistent that the library accommodate our needs when introducing library-wide initiatives.

4. Access Is Not the End Product of Description, It Is the Beginning

The aforementioned OCLC survey also revealed that half of all archival collections have no online presence. This was not a new problem to ponder. Even one of the earliest of all of these professional self-examinations, the 1998 Association of Research Libraries (ARL) survey of special collections,⁹ revealed a serious problem—that many of our most precious research materials were uncataloged and unfindable. When Judith Panitch's summary of the ARL survey results was released in 2001, the unprecedented view of special collections access, use, preservation, organizational structure, and budgets was more than enough to prompt the now-famous symposium entitled "Building on Strength: Developing an ARL Agenda for Special Collections," held at Brown University in June of 2001.¹⁰ David Stam set the tone with his keynote, "So What's So Special," Stam demanded that

> our special collections must be democratized, they must overcome their exclusionary origins..., must shed their image of aloofness..., must get their precious treasures and scholarly ephemera into the sometimes dirty hands of potential users, must place a higher priority on access to unprocessed material, and must build a wider audience including the traditional scholar..., the innovator in new uses of old stuff, and most importantly for survival, the inquiring student.¹¹

Stam went on to challenge curators and administrators alike to alter radically the nature and approach to special collections. With a single sentence, he launched a decade-long focus on hidden collections: "Make access happen—the amount of unprocessed material, much of it unique, documented in the survey is reprehensible."¹²

In response to the discussions that unfolded during the Brown Special Collections Symposium, ARL formed a Special Collections Task Force comprising special collections librarians, archivists, and library directors. The charge was to advance the agenda that had emerged at Brown and to identify and address issues of shared concern. The Task

Force addressed (and still is addressing) in various fashions the core competencies of special collections librarians, the issues of preservation, the "nineteenth-century problem," and the issue of born-digital materials, among other concerns.

At the forefront of all the issues stood the vexing problem of cataloging backlogs and unprocessed collections. The Task Force responded with a committee, headed by Barbara M. Jones, which produced a white paper in June 2003. The final product, *Hidden Collections, Scholarly Barriers: Creating Access to Unprocessed Special Collections Materials in North America's Research Libraries*,[13] has shaped the discussion of hidden collections ever since. Indeed, many of the solutions launched during the past decade point directly to the suggestions fomented by the ARL White Paper.

The landscape was bleak in 2003. The summary quite correctly detailed that uncataloged or underprocessed collections are vulnerable to duplication and theft, and they are inaccessible to the community of scholars for whom they are acquired. By their very nature, hidden collections are staff-dependent, and are excluded from library-wide preservation, retrospective conversion, and digitization efforts. When combined with the perceived "exceptional" nature of special collections materials, this led to a failure to protect and promote these scholarly resources.

It was a signal to make major changes in our approach to hidden collections. In the future, we will recognize the need to move away from a model that fashions special approaches for special materials, and instead alter our entire approach to processing so that these materials become part of the overall workflow. This means establishing system-wide workflows and processes that are sustainable and scalable.

The same view could be focused on digitization as a means of "unhiding" collections, but this too requires pressure to move away from boutique-style presentations to a larger scale that employs major discovery systems. Perhaps now is the time to consider seriously digitization prior to description. There are strong indications that the nature of the materials that will be entering the research libraries in years to come will increasingly fall outside the norms of format and description—born-digital collections, material culture collections, and new media formats and technologies. They will remain problematic for us if we persist in separating them from the whole of the library's collection. In essence, we need to recognize that we have defined many of these collections as falling outside standard procedure and have therefore turned them into problems. We have reached a moment when we need to own both the problem and the solution.

5. It Is Hard to Finish Something That Has Not Been Started

We have all learned this along the way, I expect. The collection that we bring in with the best of intentions to develop a processing plan, only to have it linger in a backlog. The bright shiny collection of books that was too hard to pass up may have no great likelihood of entering any kind of workflow. I inherited quite a massive backlog when I arrived at the Library of Congress. Serious staff time was redirected toward an arrearage project that made some headway through the undocumented collections. But when the program came to an end, I still had a backlog to face—one that I have to confess I am likely adding to as I make acquisition decisions based on the collection's needs rather than on processing realities. Sometimes it is just hard to say no. In the face of this, many of us have learned to drop our standards and at least get something started—an online finding list, a collection level record, a PDF of the dealer's inventory—to begin the process of description.

Digitization has been useful here. LC's rare book collection of 18,000 broadsides, filed with almost no cataloging whatsoever, was digitized as a collection in 1998–2000. The minimal metadata required for display eliminated the need for further cataloging. The entire text of each broadside was simply keystroked, providing us with an online catalog of posters and documents that were completely keyword searchable and easily located. LC has also experimented with crowdsourcing. Unlike Sarah Thomas's experience with maximum access, where procedures thwarted the efforts of volunteers (see chapter 16), LC posted a collection of wartime color photographs with an open invitation to tag as one desired. While many photos of wartime weapons plants and bases were identified and named, the process was grossly incomplete. We were left with photos tagged in a wild variety of interests—from the make of the car in the background to the persistent tagging of all the photos of women factory workers that displayed blood red nail polish. It was a start, I suppose. Perhaps the larger lesson learned is that we need to get it started somehow before we can build and elaborate on more complete collection description.

Why Are Special Collections Important? Exploring the Value Proposition

In March of 2009, the ARL Working Group on Special Collections released its report to the ARL Research, Teaching, and Learning Committee. Entitled "Special Collections in ARL Libraries,"[14] the report addressed several conceptual and practical issues concerning managing and administering special collections within a research library context. While the report stayed fairly close to its specific charge of addressing hidden collections and the collecting of digital and other new media, it nonetheless gave rise to the opportunity to assess the larger question of the role of special collections in the twenty-first century library.

This lens captured a new image of special collections, one vastly different from that of earlier generations. Although perhaps not surprising to many readers of this chapter, the report indicated that special collections had moved to the core of research libraries, especially in their efforts to build and support collaborative integration and enduring access to comprehensive research collections. In the old model, each research library stood as a nearly self-contained access point, and whatever was needed for research was contained within the individual library. In that model, special collections and archives were but one offering on a rather large menu. Today, research libraries are intertwined, plugged into a network that provides resources and materials virtually. Physical presence is not necessary, nor, in many cases, is the actual ownership of the materials. We have moved to an information provider model. In *this* scenario, special collections emerge as one of the few assets that distinguishes or characterizes a particular library and adds value to the educational and research experience offered by our own institution.

The value here is not limited to the unique nature of special collections holdings, although that is certainly one aspect of their value. More importantly, they represent and signify the value of the physical object. At the center of an increasingly virtual world of research stands the tribute to the power and importance of material culture. The value of these resources cuts across all levels of the academic geography. Locally, special collections represent unparalleled opportunities for teaching and research, and the predominant push to provide access and outreach to special collections speaks to this. Special collections also respond to academic programs and stand as an attribute of an institution's effort to attract faculty and spark new avenues of research. At a broad, cooperative level, it allows us to work together to create and unify astounding research opportunities—from the Roman de la Rose Digital Library[15] to the World Digital Library,[16] we have the opportunity to build collections in the virtual world that would be unimaginable in a physical setting. Just think what that allows us to do for our library, our institution, and our researchers.

What Is the Future of Special Collections?

The special collections operation of the future will successfully carry forward these lessons learned: that collections must address the academic program, we must redefine our notion of a constituency to be more expansive and global, we must embrace the entire realm of documentation, and we must adopt a more fluid and flexible system of processing and description. I envision, or at least hope for, something bold and perhaps even unfamiliar that may take a leaf from the book of current thinking on how to transform the larger research library into a modern center of research and information.

Over the last year, two major libraries put forward bold plans to reenvision the entire notion of the library as a place, as a collection, and as a conveyor of services. The New York Public Library reorganization was built around the reuse of the famed main research library—the Schwarzman Building on 42nd and Fifth. The plan called for the removal of book collections to make way for a drastic physical reworking of the historic building, thus creating a new space for a newly conceived reader. The plan envisioned the library less as a building for collections than it was the modern locus of service and access.

At the Library of Congress, the i900 plan called for the reconceptualization of the Main Reading Room as a "Center of Knowledge," the hub around which all types of access and reference services would move, unencumbered by physical or disciplinary barriers. The plan proposed to consolidate several major reading rooms into one, freeing nearly 500 staff members to step into newly revised jobs. Reference services would consolidate, staff would relocate (and in some instances be dispersed) and become free to roam the Center to provide on-the-spot service and access.

For various and differing reasons, both plans failed to launch and were set aside. They nevertheless were based on certain observations that are proven to be true and are applicable to special collections. They certainly offer a clue as to what we can expect to hear in forthcoming conversations about the role and nature of the modern research library. Similar suppositions, reworked for own experience, should inform our own thinking about the future of special collections. They can be summarized as follows:

- Expectations from technology are high and volatile.
- New information systems must be comprehensive, current, customized, compatible, convenient, and controlled (authoritative, structured, accurate, etc.).
- Language barriers are breaking down.
- Geography is no longer destiny.
- Problem solving is transdisciplinary.
- Collaboration speeds the time for innovation.
- Information is social (not solitary).
- Sources of knowledge are diverse and distributed.
- Standards and standard practices are disparate and liquid.
- With advances in technology there will be a corresponding "dematerialization." For example, if a cell phone has an app for a specific function, the item that used to perform that function will disappear.
- Digital reading is multilinear and discontinuous. In a web environment, text boundaries are no longer obvious, and in a sense the entire Web is one enormous, interconnected text.

The notion of locating a collection at the center of a service point is, of course, the description of most current special collections operations. There are a few exceptions, perhaps, where entire collections are held in remote storage and must be retrieved on time schedules, or where collections are separately located by format. Jay Satterfield's campaign to restore the collections to campus is a perfect example of the compelling power of this model. But by and large, most university and independent operations are built around this traditional model. While we are increasingly seeing space-planning decisions that remove collections from the general library to create social space, I expect that special collections will be somewhat buffered from this onslaught.

In an era where more and more libraries are actually divesting themselves of physical books, it is likely that special collections will become the central depository for all traditional formats—perhaps even without regard to scarcity and value. And as other operations disperse, the possibility that special collections will continue to build on a model of the "research center," a singular location in which we can service materials.

As for what was referred to as the twin virtue of possessing the material object and its virtual counterpart, we will be called upon to develop techniques by which we can fluidly mix the presentation of physical objects with virtual representations. As we increasingly offer a menu of choices among digital objects, online data, and the material object, we will likely develop a mechanism for delivering all of these to a researcher. I envision electronic tabletops for the reading room, with computer access and digital display easily transmitted and manipulated at the table by the researcher. It is also likely that we will be carrying with us some pad-like device that provides access to the entirety of our digital offerings, allowing us to roam freely throughout the library, bringing collections to researchers as needed and making the collections and services mobile.

Regardless of our vision for the special collections of the future, one aspect of the field must remain constant and at the forefront. Library and archival degree programs have ably demonstrated that they cannot be all things to all librarians. It is true now, more so than ever, that significant aspects of the training of special collections librarians take place in the field. While there has always been a certain apprenticeship quality to entry-level jobs, we now know that this alone is insufficient to cover the needs of the practice. Archivists are facing enormously complicated issues with born-digital materials and raw data. Media of all stripes—from sound recordings to email—now fall into our purview. Special collections are pushed in every new direction of research and documentation. Traditional rare book librarians have few opportunities to hone their skills, and their circle of like-minded colleagues on campus is diminishing as more and more faculty in history and English eschew bibliography and description for alternative methodologies.

Of course Rare Book School and similar undertakings have developed into viable alternatives, with the added benefit of their offering of curricula that heavily emphasize the craft of rare books, archives, and certain forms of electronic records. The range of courses is impressive, a perfect opportunity to sharpen skills or pick up fluency in a less familiar area. However, Rare Book School is not a degree program in itself—it is an important alternative adjunct to established programs, but it cannot stand alone. The fundamental skills of working with antiquarian books—a knowledge of paper, printing, typography, and binding—will diminish. And if we move to a roster of librarians with hybrid and hyphenated skill sets, as I imagine will be the case, then the traditional curatorial position for rare books will likely alter as well.

Do I worry needlessly here? In the History of the Book course that John Buchtel and I teach at Rare Book School, we see a constant flow of candidates who are reference or subject specialist librarians who have suddenly inherited responsibility for their library's special collections department. These are well-trained academic librarians, who in many cases haven't an inkling as to how to approach, interpret, develop, or care for a collection of rare books. We know at least anecdotally that it is difficult to find experienced rare book librarians and catalogers to fill vacancies in senior positions while at the same time we have a cluster of new librarians clamoring for some entry-level access to the field. Recent budget concerns have trimmed staffing to new lows, casting aside opportunities for entry-level training or advancement. In my own shop I am currently functioning with a staff nearly half the size of the one I inherited in 1998.

Given the current financial picture for universities and major institutions, it is unlikely that we will see an infusion of a large number of staff in special collections in the near future. Instead, we will do more with less. The special collections of the future will be a more loosely organized team of staff, many of whom hold hybrid jobs such as data archivist or imaging specialist. Certain areas of subject expertise will be covered by affiliated staff, individuals employed elsewhere in the library who possess subject or technical background that can be of assistance in terms of collection development and reference in special collections. In the Library of Congress's Rare Book Division, for example, one of our Digitization Specialists is also the curator of our LGBT collections and oversees our poetry collections, including the Poets Laureate Collection and the Archive of the Poetry Project at St. Mark's. As modern collection-building absorbs more and more contemporary materials in a variety of formats, it will become more and more difficult to have numerous collection-specific staff whose sole responsibility is the administration of a single collection. We will move away from a fixed notion of staffing to a team of affiliated staff members, building a circle of support around the primary staff.

Moving from the Present to the Future

The problem with these kinds of predictive talks is that we have little upon which to base our suppositions other than current trends and a nostalgic retrospective examination of whence we have come. Truth be told, the only thing we can do is point to the constants and imagine how they will translate in a new environment. I signed on to my first full-time job in special collections in 1979; my first professional position was in 1983. There was no way imaginable in that year that I could have predicted the landscape of the present. The personal computer was still a few years off, shared computer data was in its infancy, and the world was comfortably analog. More than three decades later, the only aspects of my daily work life that correspond to the past are the principal tasks. And perhaps that is the point of all of this. The future of special collections will be determined by the decision as to whether the current core values of our work remain intact—to build collections that support research and instruction, to interpret these collections to our constituency, and to work to preserve and protect them. And perhaps more poetically, will we continue to value the reverence and the passion for the material object, working to keep its meaning and story alive?

I attended my first RBMS conference in 1984 in Austin, Texas. It was a different time; conferences were much smaller and more intimate. The room was filled with librarians who were already established in the field—they were, in essence, responsible for creating the profession of special collections librarianship. My generation's task, I suppose, was to solidify and expand the reach of our field. Peter Hanff of The Bancroft Library introduced me to a crowd of librarians at the opening reception—Sam Streit (director of the John Hay Library at Brown University), Daniel Traister (curator of the Department of Special Collections at the University of Pennsylvania), and Peter Van Wingen (who was then at the Rare Books and Special Collections Division of the Library of Congress). I was thunderstruck. Of course I knew who they were. They were like the gods. And indeed they and their cohorts had shaped our field, written about our practices, implemented new programs, and formed the very notion of what it meant to be a special collections librarian.

Now some thirty years later I will not presume to say that we have taken their place, for today we move about in a much bigger space, with greater fluidity, fostering a variety of skills and interests, but it has been my generation's turn to ponder the future of the profession. Only a few years ago we were holding committee meetings, addressing the "greying" of the profession and succession planning—a concern that now seems silly given the massive audience at RBMS of over 400 attendees. I remember when 200 people was a nearly unachievable target. So our fears have been quelled.

I will say this. In that crowd is the next generation of our field. They have the passion. They seem to have the right combination of smarts and sass. I even find the tattoos promising. They *already* live in a world different from ours, with new skills and unimaginable dreams of what is to come. No need to question the future of special collections. They are here among us. Bring it on!

NOTES

1. Jackie M. Dooley and Katherine Luce, *Taking Our Pulse: The OCLC Research Survey of Special Collections and Archives* (Dublin, OH: OCLC Research, 2010). The full report is available at www.oclc.org/content/dam/research/publications/library/2010/2010-11.pdf.
2. Ibid., 9.
3. More information about this collection can be found at www.lib.umich.edu/islamic/.

4. More information about this collection and the Hidden Collections project at Lehigh University can be found at http://digital.lib.lehigh.edu/hidden/.
5. More information about this collection and the Hidden Collections project at the Newberry Library can be found at http://publications.newberry.org/french pamphlets/?page_id=7.
6. More information about this project at the Smithsonian can be found at www.mnh.si.edu/rc/fieldbooks/.
7. More information about this collection can be found at www.asu.edu/lib/archives/chicano.htm.
8. More information about this collection can be found at www.litchfieldhistoricalsociety.org/archon/?p=collections/controlcard&id=783.
9. Judith M. Panitch, *Special Collections in ARL Libraries: Results of the 1998 Survey Sponsored by the ARL Research Collections Committee* (Washington, DC: Association of Research Libraries, 2001), www.arl.org/storage/documents/publications/special-collections-arl-libraries.pdf.
10. The agenda and selected presentations from the symposium can be found under the title "The Unique Role of Special Collections—Building on Strength: Developing an ARL Agenda for Special Collections," www.arl.org/storage/documents/publications/building-on-strength-developing-an-arl-agenda-for-special-collections-june2001.pdf.
11. David Stam, "So What's So Special?" in *The Unique Role of Special Collections—Building on Strength: Developing an ARL Agenda for Special Collections* (Washington, DC: Association of Research Libraries, 2001), 7.
12. Stam, 11.
13. Barbara M. Jones and Nicole Bouche, *Hidden Collections, Scholarly Barriers: Creating Access to Unprocessed Special Collections Materials in North America's Research Libraries: A White Paper for the Association of Research Libraries Task Force on Special Collection* (United States: [publisher not identified], 2003).
14. "Special Collections in ARL Libraries: A Discussion Report from the ARL Working Group on Special Collections," (Washington, DC: Association of Research Libraries, 2009), www.arl.org/bm~doc/scwg-report.pdf.
15. The Roman de la Rose Digital Library "is a joint project of the Sheridan Libraries of Johns Hopkins University and the Bibliothèque nationale de France…to create an online library of all manuscripts containing the thirteenth-century poem Roman de la Rose." As of August 2015 there were "digital surrogates of more than 130 Roman de la Rose manuscripts" and the collection planned to continue to grow, http://romandelarose.org.
16. As of August 2015, World Digital Library's website (www.wdl.org/en/) stated that one could "search 12,214 items about 193 countries between 1200 BCE and 2000 CE."

About the Editors and Contributors

Melissa A. Hubbard is the Head of Special Collections and Archives at Kelvin Smith Library, Case Western Reserve University. She previously served as the Rare Book Librarian at Southern Illinois University. Her research and professional interests include the pedagogical uses of special collections materials and innovative approaches to exposing hidden collections.

Robert H. Jackson is a senior partner at Kohrman Jackson & Krantz, PLL in Cleveland, and is also a noted writer, speaker, and collector of rare books and art. Jackson's broad knowledge of, and involvement in, bibliophilic endeavors are reflected in his affiliations with such organizations as the Grolier Club, the Rowfant Club of Cleveland, Association Internationale de Bibliophile (Paris), and the Fellowship of American Bibliophilic Societies, of which he is a founder and past chairman. At Case Western Reserve University, Jackson serves as chair of the Baker-Nord Committee for Humanities Advisory Board, is a member of the Visiting Committee for the College of Arts and Sciences, and the Institute for the Science of Origins Visiting Committee. He is the Distinguished Visiting Scholar at Kelvin Smith Library.

Arnold Hirshon has been the Associate Provost and University Librarian at Case Western Reserve University since August 2010. Hirshon has an extensive scholarly record that includes many monographs, among them the *Library Strategic Planning Toolkit* (with Stephen Spohn), and *Outsourcing Library Technical Services* (with Barbara Winters). He is also the author of numerous articles about strategic management, organizational design, technology, leadership, information service integration, assessment and optimization of operations, and nonprofit management. A frequent lecturer nationally and internationally, Hirshon has given lectures in nearly forty countries on six continents on a wide range of topics, including organizational management, trend spotting and analysis, technology planning, and operations assessment and optimization.

About the Editors and Contributors

Tom Congalton founded Between the Covers Rare Books in 1985; the firm specializes in literary first editions, archives and manuscripts, and general rare books. He served as President of the Antiquarian Booksellers' Association of America from 2000 to 2002, and as President of the International League of Antiquarian Booksellers (ILAB) from 2012 to 2014. He has taught at both Rare Book School in Charlottesville, VA, and at the Colorado Antiquarian Booksellers Seminar.

Daniel De Simone is the Eric Weinmann Librarian at the Folger Shakespeare Library. As Librarian, De Simone is responsible for the operations of the Central Library and in coordination with other Directors, the management of the institution. He came to the Folger from his position as Curator of the Lessing J. Rosenwald Collection in the Rare Book and Special Collections Division at the Library of Congress. Before his appointment as Rosenwald Curator, De Simone owned his own bookselling business that he operated for twenty-two years in New York City.

Mark Dimunation was appointed Chief of the Rare Book and Special Collections Division, Library of Congress, in March 1998. As Chief, Dimunation is responsible for the development and management of the Rare Book Collection, the largest collection of rare books in North America. He acquires materials, develops programs of lectures and presentations, and oversees the operations of the Division. He specializes in eighteenth- and nineteenth-century English and American printing and has considerable experience working with antiquarian materials as well as fine press and contemporary artists' books.

Stephen Enniss is Director of the Harry Ransom Center. Before coming to The University of Texas, he held previous appointments at the Folger Shakespeare Library and at Emory University's Manuscript, Archives, and Rare Book Library. His own research interests are in twentieth-century poetry, and he has written on Ted Hughes, Sylvia Plath, and Seamus Heaney, among other figures. He is the author, most recently, of *After the Titanic: A Life of Derek Mahon*.

About the Editors and Contributors

E. Haven Hawley is Chair of the Special and Area Studies Collections Department at George A. Smathers Libraries at the University of Florida. She has been program director at the Immigration History Research Center and taught the history of science as visiting faculty at the University of Minnesota. A heritage professional and specialist in printing technologies, she holds a PhD in the history and sociology of technology and science from the Georgia Institute of Technology.

Christoph Irmscher is Provost Professor of English at Indiana University Bloomington and George F. Getz Jr. Professor in the Wells Scholars Program, which he also directs. Among his books are *The Poetics of Natural History; Longfellow Redux; Private Poet, Public Man: Henry Wadsworth Longfellow at 200;* and *Louis Agassiz: Creator of American Science.* He is the editor of the Library of America edition of John James Audubon's *Writings and Drawings*. He has just completed a biography of the writer, editor, and political activist Max Eastman. His award-winning bicentennial Longfellow exhibit can be found at http://hcl.harvard.edu/libraries/houghton/exhibits/longfellow/.

Athena N. Jackson provides leadership, coordination, and oversight for many of the day-to-day operations of the Special Collections Library at the University of Michigan, especially those centered on services for readers and management of collections. Most recently, she was Special Collections Librarian at the University of Miami. She has also worked in the electronic publishing industry, where she was responsible for digital humanities collections for academic research. She is an active member of the Rare Books and Manuscripts Section of the American Library Association. She has spoken nationally on diversity in the special collections profession and on access to historical newspapers.

Selby Kiffer is the international senior specialist for books and manuscripts at Sotheby's, where he has worked for more than thirty years.

Jim Kuhn is the Joseph N. Lambert and Harold B. Schleifer Director of Rare Books, Special Collections, and Preservation at the University of Rochester River Campus Libraries. He has master's degrees in library science and philosophy from Kent State University. Prior to the University of Rochester, Kuhn oversaw acquisitions, cataloging, technical services, and photography at the Folger Shakespeare Library, where he last served as Interim Eric Weinmann Librarian. His publications include the forthcoming "'A Hawk from a Handsaw:' Collating Possibilities with The Shakespeare Quartos Archive," in *New Technologies and Renaissance Studies,* eds. Tassie Gniady, Kris McAbee, and Jessica C. Murphy.

Ken Lopez began his bookselling career at the Goddard College bookstore in Plainfield, Vermont, in the 1970s when Raymond Carver was teaching in Goddard's MFA program. After 1978 publishing industry changes, Lopez began issuing catalogs of modern literary first editions by contemporary, living, working writers in 1981, inadvertently helping to create a field that came to be known as "hypermodern" book collecting. Buying and selling living writers' works led directly to helping sell those writers' manuscripts and literary archives, which Lopez has been doing since the early 1990s, and which now forms a major part of his rare book business.

Paul Ruxin (1943–2016) was a retired Senior Partner of the international law firm Jones, Day. He was a member of the Caxton Club of Chicago, the Rowfant Club of Cleveland, the Club of Odd Volumes of Boston, and the Grolier Club of New York. He was the immediate past chairman of the Board of Governers of the Folger Shakespeare Library, a former member of the Board of Trustees of the Poetry Foundation, and a member of the Boards of the Newberry Library and The American Writers Museum, as well as a Governor of Dr. Johnson's House.

Jay Satterfield is the head of Dartmouth College's Rauner Special Collections Library. He received his PhD in American Studies from the University of Iowa in 1999, and is the author of *"The World's Best Books": Taste, Culture and the Modern Library.*

Alice Schreyer is Vice President for Collections and Library Services at the Newberry Library. Her previous positions include Associate University Librarian for Area Studies and Special Collections and Curator of Rare Books at the University of Chicago Library and Assistant Library Director for Special Collections, University of Delaware Library. Schreyer taught "Special Collections Librarianship" at Rare Book School, University of Virginia. She is the author of *Education and Training for Careers in Special Collections Librarianship* (Association for Research Libraries, 2004) and a past Chair of the Rare Book School Board of Directors and the Rare Books and Manuscripts Section of ACRL/ALA.

Joel Silver is Director of the Lilly Library, Indiana University Bloomington, where he has worked since 1983. He has published a number of articles on rare books and book collecting in *AB Bookman's Weekly* and *Fine Books and Collections Magazine,* and has taught courses in many subjects related to rare books at the Department of Information and Library Science at Indiana University, where he serves as the Director of the Special Collections Specialization.

Sarah Thomas is Vice President for the Harvard Library and the Roy E. Larsen Librarian of Harvard College. From 2007 to 2013 she served as Bodley's Librarian, overseeing Oxford's university libraries, including the historic Bodleian Library. In 2007 she received the Melvil Dewey Award from the American Library Association, and in 2004 she served as the president of the Association of Research Libraries. In 2010 she was elected a member of Oxford's University Council. She is a member of the RLUK Board of Directors.

Index

A

ABC of Reading (Pound), 134
academic program, special collections responding to, 170–171
access to special collections
   cataloging backlogs and unprocessed collections preventing, 175–177
   historical overview of, 157–165
   hybrid access to print and online holdings, 17
Accetta, Giula, 80
"Acknowledging the Past, Forging the Future" (colloquium on special collections), xiii, xv, 21, 46, 53, 64, 94
"Acquainting the Public with Rare Books" (conference session), 168
acquisitions
   donor relations, 21–23
   gifts-in-kind, 11–20
   print collections, building and maintaining distinctive, 15–20
active learning (exuberant chaos), 124–128, 132–154
Adventures of Huckleberry Finn (Twain), 51, 109
affinities and alliances, new tools for building, 14–15
Agassiz, Louis, 133, 134
age of book collectors, 90
Aguinaldo, Emilio, 145–146
AIDS Education Posters, 22
Alice's Adventures in Wonderland (Carroll), 33
All in the Family (television show), 142
Allen, Peter, 73
American Library Association, 69
American Writers Museum, 49
Amistad Research Center (Tulane), 172
Andrew W. Mellon Foundation, 74, 158, 172
Aquinas, Thomas, 65
archive of the future, 109–110
Arizona State University, 172
ARL (Association of Research Libraries), 37, 158, 175
artifacts
   books as, 5–8
   experiencing authentic and compelling, 163
   manuscripts and, 136
   meanings of, 3–10
   reconstruction of memories and, 6–8
   scrapbooks as, 41–42
   valuing, 4
Atwater, Edward C., 22
auction house, role of, 45–51
audience, identifying and creating a new, 92–93
Austen, Jane, 111
autographs, 102–103

B

backlogs in cataloging and unprocessed collections preventing access to special collections, 175–177
Baer, Harold, 73
Baldwin, James, 146–147
The Bancroft Library, 184
Barlow, William, 33
Basbanes, Nicholas, 33
Bay Psalm Book, 50
Beauties of Swift: or, the Favorite Offspring of Wit & Genius (Swift), 48–49

Index

Belanger, Terry, 31
Belton, Don, 144
Berenson, Bernard, 148
Berenson, Mary, 144
bibliography, descriptive, 69–72
The Bibliomania: Or, Book-Madness; Containing Some Account of the History, Symptoms, and Cure of This Fatal Disease (Dibdin), 33
Black Metropolis Research Consortium, 173
Bloch, Bernard, 110
BlogSpot software, 145
Blumenthal, Joseph, 81
BOA Editions, 12
Bodleian Library, 163, 164
Boni & Liveright, 47
"Book Collecting: Personal Rewards and Public Benefits" (Barlow), 33
book collectors
  age of, 90
  demographics, 90
  as donors, 31–34
  establishing their own institution or foundation, 46
  librarians, booksellers, and private collectors working together, 92–93
  overview, 31–34
book fairs, 91
Book Traces, 16
Books and Prints, Past and Present (conference), 45
"Books and Society in History" (RBMS Preconference 1980), 168
books (physical)
  as artifacts, 5–8
  information carried by, 70–72
  monetary value of books and manuscripts, role of, 50–51
  as primary source material, 69–70
booksellers
  librarians, booksellers, and private collectors working together, 92–93

  nonbook materials and, 86–88
  and technology, 85–86
The Book Collector, 33
born-digital content, 106–113, 176, 181–182
Boswell, James, 101, 107
Bowden, Mary, 147
Bowers, Fredson, 70
British Library, 31, 106, 162
broadsides, 5, 177
brochures and marketing materials, 96–97
Brown University, 159, 170, 175, 184
Buchtel, John, 182
Buffalo Public Library, 51
"Building on Strength: Developing an ARL Agenda for Special Collections" (symposium), 175
building special collections, 48, 67–69, 77–78, 90, 183. *See also* collection development

C

Calatrava, Santiago, 69
Campbell, Joseph, 97
careers in special collection librarianship, 82–83
"The Care of Rare Books" (conference session), 168
Carini, Peter, 118
Carroll, Lewis, 135, 136–139
case study
  community-based collections, 39–43
  digital scholarship trends, trajectory of career as case study for present and future, 55–59
Case Western Reserve University (CWRU), xiii, 39–43, 49, 89, 91, 94
cataloging backlogs and unprocessed collections preventing access to special collections, 175–177
Cataloging Hidden Special Collections and Archives program (CLIR), 158–159, 172

Cather, Willa, 88
Center for the Book (Library of
  Congress), 67
Chardin, Teilhard de, 100
Charles Scribner, 47
*Chronicle of a Death Foretold (Crónica de
  una muerte anunciada)* (García
  Márquez), 104
classroom
  selection of materials for, 125
  students, relinquishing control of
    classroom experience to, 120–124
Clay, Edward William, 146
Clemens, Samuel, 102
Cleveland Play House (CPH) archives,
  39–43
CLIR (Council on Library and
  Information Resources), 74, 158,
  172
Coetzee, J. M., 103, 110
collaboration between and within
  institutions, 172–173
"Collecting Scientific Literature"
  (conference session), 168
collection development. *See also* building
  special collections
  collaborative collection development,
    open, formal, publicly
    documented, 17–20
  policies for, 13–14
  print collections, building and
    maintaining distinctive, 15–20
  starting the process of collection
    description, importance of,
    177–178
Colorado Book Seminar, 91
community-based collections
  case study, 39–43
  defined, 37
  importance of, 38–39
  integration into research institutions,
    43–44
  overview, 37–38

role of, 38–39
Complete Works of Walt Whitman
  (Whitman), 102–103
computer-generated manuscripts,
  103–107
"Computers and Rare Books: An
  Introductory Session" (conference
  session), 168
Congalton, Tom, 85, 188
ContentDM, 126
copyright issues, 22, 73–74, 111–112, 126
Cornell Human Sexuality Collection, 19
Cornell University, 163, 171
Cornell University Library, 31
correspondence
  email, 107–109, 111, 112
  letters, 97–98
Costelloe, Frank, 148
Crone, Frank, 145–146, 147
*Crónica de una muerte anunciada
  (Chronicle of a Death Foretold)*
  (García Márquez), 104
crowdsourcing, 177
curatorial boundaries, crossing, 119–123
current core values of work in special
  collections, 183
cut-and-paste manuscripts, 95

D

Dacier, Anne, 79
Dartmouth College, 48, 117–129
Darwin, Charles, 46–47
database, creation of searchable full-text,
  73–74
Davies, Robertson, 33
Dawn (Dreiser), 135
De Simone, Daniel, xiii, 89, 188
demographics of book collectors, 90
Dennis, John, 78
Department of Special Collections
  (University of Pennsylvania), 184
descriptive bibliography, 69–72
Deshon, Florence, 135

Index

Dibdin, Thomas Frognall, 33
Dickinson, Emily, 140, 141
digital archives, 98, 108, 110–113
digital scholarship, 53–59, 75, 101–113
digital storage media, 105–107
digitization of materials, 54–59, 74–75, 125–127, 169–170, 177
Dimunation, Mark, xiii, 67, 164, 167, 188
donors
    book collectors as, 31–34
    potential donors, identifying and encouraging, 31–32
    relations with, 21–23
Donovan, Mary, 131
Dooley, Jackie, 171
Doren, Carl Van, 45
Dreiser, Theodore, 135
duality of structure, 9
The Dunciad (Pope), 71
Dunn, Marilyn, 160
Dupont, Christian, 15
Dwinelle, John Whipple, 11
Dylan, Bob, 48

E

EAST (Eastern Academic Scholars' Trust), 18
Eastman, George, 18
Eastman, Max, 133, 135
ECCO (Eighteenth Century Collections Online), 70
EEBO (Early English Books Online), 70
Einstein, Albert, 167
El amor en los tiempos del cólera (Love in the Time of Cholera) (García Márquez), 104, 105
Eliasson, Olafur, 118, 127
Ellison, Robert Spurrier, 135
email correspondence, 107–109, 111, 112
Emancipation Proclamation, 48
Emory University, 172
Empson, William, 137
Encyclopedia Arctica, 125–126
"Enemies of Books: Revisited" (RBMS Preconference 1983), 168
Eng-L 460 Modern Literary Archives (syllabus), 150–154
Enniss, Stephen, 53, 101, 188
ethical and practical principles of working with modern literary archives, 132–154
evolution of a writer's work, 95–96
"The Evolution of the Concept of Special Collections in American Research Libraries" (Joyce), 38
exhibition tour of Bay Psalm Book, 50
exuberant chaos (active learning), 124–128, 132–154

F

Ferber, Becky, 142
"Five Theses on the Future of Special Collections" (Overholt), 38
Fleeman, Richard, 70
Fleming, Ian, 33, 142
Flickr, 159
Flickr Commons, 162
Flinn, Gallagher, 80
Florida Polytechnic University (FPU), 69
Folger Shakespeare Library, 92, 110
Frankfurter, Marion, 132
Fred W. Smith National Library for the Study of George Washington at Mount Vernon, 49
"From 'Treasure Room' to 'School Room': Special Collections and Education" (Smith), 38
full-text database, creation of searchable, 73–74
Furniss, Harry, 135, 136–138
future of special collections (overview), 179–184
Fyner, Konrad, 11

Index

G

GAGV (Gay Alliance of the Genesee Valley), 19
García Márquez, Gabriel, 103–105
Gaskell, Philip, 70
A Gentle Madness (Basbanes), 33
George Eastman House International Museum of Photography and Film, 17, 18–19
"Getting There From Here: Setting the Agenda for Special Collections in the 21st Century" (RBMS Preconference 1996), 169
Ghosh, Anjona, 142
Gibbons, Susan, 20
Giddens, Anthony, 9
gifts-in-kind, 11–15
Giroux, Robert, 45
Goodwin, Jonathan, 47
Google Books, 70, 80, 82, 173
Gordon Hall and Grace Hoag Collection of Dissenting and Extremist Propaganda (Brown University), 159
Gottschlich, Michelle, 144, 147–149
Gould, Stephen J., xv
Greek Word Study Tool of the Perseus Digital Library, 82
GreenGlass service, 16–17
Guffey, Don Carlos, 47
Gutenberg Bible, 49

H

Hagan, Malcolm E., 49
Hale, Everett, 138, 140, 141
Hanff, Peter, 184
Harold A. Kanthor Collection of Gilbert and Sullivan, 21
Harry Ransom Center (The University of Texas), 32, 102, 105, 108
Harvard Business School, 32
HathiTrust, 16–17, 70, 73, 173
Hawley, E. Haven, 3, 189

Hemingway, Ernest, 47
hidden collections, 158–159, 172–173, 175–177
Hidden Collections, Scholarly Barriers: Creating Access to Unprocessed Special Collections Materials in North America's Research Libraries (Jones), 176
highlight collecting, 46–49
Hirshon, Arnold, 94, 187
historical overview of access to special collections, 157–165
Homer, 76–77
Homer in Print; A Catalogue of the Bibliotheca Homerica Langiana at the University of Chicago Library, 77–78, 93
Housman, A. E., 33
Hubbard, Melissa A., 37, 187
human universe, 99–100
Hunting for Hope (Sanders), 142
hybrid access to print and online holdings, 17

I

ILAB (International League of Antiquarian Booksellers), 91
The Iliad (Homer), 77, 78–79
IMLS (Institute for Museum and Library Studies), 83
Imprints and Impressions: Milestones in Human Progress (exhibition catalog), 93
in-kind donations. *See* gifts-in-kind
incunable books, 65
Indiana University Bloomington, 132–133
information carried by physical books, 70–72
intangibles, preservation of, 95–100
integration into research institutions, community-based collections, 43–44
Ireland, Samuel, 101

197

Index

Ireland, William, 101
Ireland forgeries, 101
Irmscher, Christoph, 131, 189
"Issues, Strategies and Opportunities" (RBMS Preconference 1990), 169

J
Jackson, Athena N., 53, 189
Jackson, Gardner, 132
Jackson, Robert H., xiii, 67, 94, 187
Jenns, Erika, 142, 144
John Hay Library (Brown University), 184
Johnson, Samuel, 48, 79, 110
Jones, Barbara M., 176
Jones, Megan, 132
Joyce, William L., 38

K
Kanthor, Harold, 21
Kelvin Smith Library (Case Western Reserve University), xiii
Kennedy, Robert, 48
Keogh, Andrew, 66
Kesey, Ken, 97
Kiffer, Selby, 45, 189
Kroch Library (Cornell University), 163
Kuhn, Jim, 11, 190

L
Lamperly, Paul, 33
Lang, Michael, 76–80, 81, 93, 171
Lattimore, Richmond, 7
Lawrence, T. E., 81
Lehigh University, 172
Lewis and Clark expedition official report, 46–47
librarians
  booksellers, librarians, and private collectors working together, 92–93
  careers in special collection librarianship, 82–83
  staffing issues, 182–183
  training for special collections librarians, 181–182
Library of Congress, 67, 94, 177, 179–180, 183, 184
library-wide initiatives, participating in, 173–174
Light, Michelle, 126
"Like A Rolling Stone" (Dylan), 48
Lilly Library (Indiana University Bloomington), 31, 132–154
Lincoln, Abraham, 48
Lindseth, Jon A., 31, 68
Litchfield Historical Society, 172
literary archives, practical and ethical principles of working with modern, 132–154
The Lives of the Most Eminent English Poets (Johnson), 79
Longfellow, Henry Wadsworth, 133
Lopez, Ken, 85, 95, 190
Love in the Time of Cholera (El amor en los tiempos del cólera) (García Márquez), 104, 105
Luce, Katherine, 171

M
Magna Carta, 50
"Mainstream or Margin? How Others View Special Collections" (RBMS Preconference 1993), 169
manuscript collectors establishing their own institution or foundation, 46
manuscripts
  computer-generated, 103–107
  cut-and-paste, 95
  monetary value of books and manuscripts, role of, 50–51
  paintings as competition with, 49
  as physical objects, 136–137
  types of, 149
Mark Twain Project Online, 109
marketing materials and brochures, 96–97
Marshall, Marty, 32

Index

McCarthy, Molly, 144
McEwan, Ian, 108–109
McGann, Jerome, 75
McKenzie, D. F., 34
McLeod, Randall, 80
meanings of artifacts, 3–10
Melville, Herman, 47
memories, reconstruction of, 6–8
Metilli, Daniele, 80, 81, 82, 83
Meyer, Tobias, 49
Moby-Dick (Melville), 46–47
modern literary archives, practical and ethical principles of working with, 132–154
Modern Literary Archives Eng-L 460 (syllabus), 150–154
modern research library
 role and nature of, 179–181
 special collections role in, 178–179
monetary value of books and manuscripts, role of, 50–51
MONK (pattern recognition and machine-learning software), 162
Monmouth County Library, 85
Morgan Library & Museum, 31
Moser, Diana, 78
Most, Glenn W., 77
Mrs. Dalloway (Woolf), 136

N

Naismith, James, 48
National Archives, 50
National Center for Textual and Lexical Resources, 82
National Endowment for the Humanities, 74
National Historic Publications & Records Committee, 74
Neville, Maurice, 47
New Bodleian Library, 164
"New Occasions, New Duties: Changing Roles and Expectations" (RBMS Preconference 2002), 169

A New Republic of Letters: Memory and Scholarship in the Age of Digital Reproduction, 75
New York Public Library, 179
Newberry Library, 68, 172
Nguyen, Ly, 146–147
NINES (Networked Infrastructure for Nineteenth-Century Electronic Scholarship), 16
nonbook materials, booksellers and, 86–88
Noosphere, 100
Normal, David, 162
NPR (National Public Radio), 161

O

OCLC (Online Computer Library Center), 159, 171
The Odyssey (Homer), 78, 79–81
Olson, Charles, 99
Omeka software, 147
Origin of Species (Darwin), 46–47
original items not representations, preservation of, 99–100
Ovenden, Richard, 160
Overholt, John, 38
Ozell, John, 79

P

PACSCL (Philadelphia Area Consortium of Special Collections Libraries), 172
paintings, antiquarian books and manuscripts as competition with, 49
Pamuk, Orhan, 32
Panitch, Judith, 175
Pappas, Elizabeth, 142
Parker, Barrington, 73
"Past Forward! Meeting Stakeholder Needs in Twenty-First Century Special Collections" (conference), 20
Patey, N., 80

Index

Patino, Bernadette, 142, 145, 147
Pawn Stars (television show), 64–65
Perseus Digital Library, 82
photographs, 98
physical books
    as artifacts, 5–8
    information carried by, 70–72
    monetary value of books and manuscripts, role of, 50–51
    as primary source material, 69–70
physical objects and virtual representations, ability to offer both, 181
Plomer, William, 142
Poe, Edgar Allan, 135
policies for collection development, 13–14
Pope, Alexander, 78–79
potential donors, identifying and encouraging, 31–32
Pottle, Frederick, 70
Pound, Ezra, 134
Powell, Lawrence Clark, 63–66
practical and ethical principles of working with modern literary archives, 132–154
primary source material
    example of students learning to use, 120–123
    physical books as, 69–70
print collections, building and maintaining distinctive, 15–20
print retention partnerships, 17–18
printers, 4–5
"Private Collectors and Special Collections Libraries" (rare book forum), xiii
Provenance Project (University of Pennsylvania), 159

R

Radcliffe Institute for Advanced Study (Harvard University), 160

Rare Book and Special Collections Division (Library of Congress), 67, 184
Rare Book Forum (Library of Congress), 67
Rare Book School (University of Virginia), 31, 82–83, 86, 182
Rauner Special Collections Library (Dartmouth College), 117–129
RBMS preconferences, 82, 168–169
RBMS (Rare Books and Manuscripts Section) of the ACRL, 82–83
"Reconsidering Libraries and Scholarship: Special Collections and New Directions in Humanities Research" (RBMS Preconference 1987), 169
reconstruction of memories and artifacts, 6–8
Reddit, 80
Reese, Bill, xiii, 67, 68
research library, modern
    role and nature of, 179–181
    special collections role in, 178–179
Reynolds, Joshua, 111
River Campus Libraries (University of Rochester), 11–23
RLUK (Research Libraries UK), 159
Rogers, Bruce, 81
Rose, Stuart, 93
Rubenstein, David, 50
Rushdie, Salman, 103, 107–108, 109, 112
Ruxin, Paul, 67, 190

S

Sager, Carol Bayer, 73
Sanders, Deborra, 144
Sanders, Scott Russell, 142
Satterfield, Jay, 38, 48, 56, 88, 117, 171, 181, 190
Schlesinger Library (Radcliffe Institute for Advanced Study at Harvard), 160–162

Index

"Scholarly Communication and the Future of Special Collections" (RBMS Preconference 1992), 169
Schreyer, Alice, xiii, 67, 73, 77, 171, 191
Scott, Alicia, 150
scrapbooks, 40–42
searchable full-text database, creation of, 73–74
Shakespeare, William, 101, 110
Shankman, Steven, 78
Shaw, George Bernard, 32
Shelley, Percy Bysshe, 163
Shufeldt, Mason Abercrombie, 142, 143, 150
signatures as coveted object, 102–103
Silver, Joel, 31, 63, 94, 191
Sinclair, Upton, 142
Small, Albert H., 33
Smith, Geoffrey, 21, 46
Smith, Steven Escar, 38
Smith, Zadie, 113
Smithsonian Institution, 161, 172
Sotheby's, 45–51
"Special Collections in ARL Libraries" (report), 178
"Special Collections in the Age of Digital Scholarship" (panel), 53, 58, 85
Special Collections Library (University of Michigan), 56
Specimen Days (Whitman), 103
Spender, Stephen, 135
Stam, David, 175
Stanford University, 172
starting the process of collection description, importance of, 177–178
Stauffer, Andrew, 16
Stefansson, Vilhjalmur, 125
Stephen, Karin Costelloe, 144, 147–149
Sterling Memorial Library (Yale University), 66
Streit, Sam, 184
students, relinquishing control of classroom experience to, 120–124
Stuff: Compulsive Hoarding and the Meaning of Things, 33
stylostatistics, 110
Summa Theologiae (Aquinas), 11, 65
The Sun Also Rises (Hemingway), 47
Sustainable Collection Services, 16
Swan, Morgan, 123
syllabus for Eng-L 460 Modern Literary Archives, 150–154
Sylvie and Bruno (Carroll), 135, 136–139
"Symposium on Authenticity of Print Materials" (Library of Congress), 91
Syracuse University, 19

T

tachygraphy, 80–81
Taking Our Pulse: The OCLC Research Survey of Special Collections and Archives, 171
Tanselle, Thomas, 70
Tatem, Jill, 44
teaching with special collections, 132–154
"Techniques of Rare Books" (conference session), 168
technology and booksellers, 85–86
Tenniel, John, 137
Theimer, Kate, 44
Thévenot, Jean Coulon de, 80–81
Thomas, Sarah, 157, 173, 177, 191
Thoreau, Henry David, 102
Tickell, Thomas, 79
The Torrents of Spring (Hemingway), 47
training for special collections librarians, 181–182
Traister, Daniel, 184
transformation in special collections (generally), 73–83, 89–94
Tulane University, 172
Twain, Mark, 51, 131

201

"The Twilight of Rare Book Collecting, or How to Stop Worrying and Love Automation" (conference session), 168

U

Uncle Tom's Cabin, 147
University of Chicago, 76–77, 79, 93
University of Chicago Library, 76
University of Chicago Press, 77
University of Dayton, 93
University of Michigan, 56, 172
University of Pennsylvania, 159, 184
University of Rochester, 11–23
University of Texas, 32
University of Toronto, 80
University of Virginia, 16, 31, 78, 82–83
unprocessed collections and cataloging backlogs preventing access to special collections, 175–177
Updike, John, 98–99, 106–107, 109
user, bringing collection to the, 171–173

V

value of special collections, 178–179
Van Wingen, Peter, 184
Vander Meulen, David, 69–72, 78
Vanzetti, Bartolomeo, 131–132, 150
Victoria State Library, 163
virtual representations and physical objects, ability to offer both, 181
Visnjic, Vanya, 80

Vonnegut, Kurt, 142

W

Walters, Annie B., 103
Washington, George, 48–49
"Western Americana" (conference session), 168
What Jane Saw (website), 111
Where Angels Fear to Tread: Descriptive Bibliography and Alexander Pope (Vander Meulen), 69
Whitall, Hannah, 148
Whitman, Sarah Helen, 135
Whitman, Walt, 51, 102–103, 136
"Will the Collector of Today Be the Donor of Tomorrow?" (Jackson), xiii
Williford, Christa, 158
Wollstonecraft, Mary, 163
Woodruff Library (Emory University), 172
Woodstock, 97–98
Woolf, Virginia, 136, 144
Worcester, Dean C., 145–146
Wray, David, 79
Wylie, Andrew, 107

Y

Yakel, Elizabeth, 15
Yale University, 20, 66, 172
Young, Neil, 99
Your House (Eliasson), 118, 127